TO

COMPTON MACKENZIE

Presented by Canon D. B. Eperson
July 1995

D. B. Eperson

THE FIRST BOOK
OF THE
GRAMOPHONE RECORD

Giving Advice upon the Selection of Fifty-odd good Records from Byrd to Beethoven, a Listener's description of their Music, the Words of the Songs (with translations where necessary), and a Glossary of Technical Terms.

BY

PERCY A. SCHOLES

SECOND EDITION
(with many changes)

OXFORD UNIVERSITY PRESS
London Edinburgh Glasgow Copenhagen
New York Toronto Melbourne Cape Town
Bombay Calcutta Madras Shanghai
Humphrey Milford
1927

Printed in England at the Oxford University Press
By John Johnson Printer to the University

CONTENTS

INTRODUCTION

ON GRAMOPHONES

A WILL recently published in the press was of interest for a reference to music. It was that of the son of a Captain Matthew Liddon, R.N., 'second in command of Sir Edward Parry's Arctic Expedition'. *He left to his son Edward, to devolve as an heirloom, the hand-organ which his father took with him on his Polar voyage.*

Which of Parry's expeditions is referred to I am not sure. Perhaps the one which set out in May 1821. The return home from this took place two and a half years later, in November 1823, and I am writing this Introduction just a century after that, in November 1923. To-day the reference to the 'hand-organ' looks pathetic. How many tunes could it play? Six, perhaps, or maybe twelve. Twelve would be a good number, and they would be ground out, wheezily enough, probably by means of paper rolls, or perhaps of metal discs or of wooden rollers with pins. The tone was probably sweet and fluty, but the tunes simple, and meagrely harmonized, as we still occasionally hear them in the streets, in the performances of the few surviving hand-organists. This was not a luxurious musical provision for a voyage of two and a half years!

I suppose that all Arctic explorers nowadays take Gramophones. In fact we may be sure that they do so. And instead of half a dozen or a dozen tunes, they can have at their disposition hundreds—even thousands. Many of the best 'tunes' of the world, played or sung by many of the best performers, await their enjoyment in the form of Gramophone Records.

A very few years ago, fine music was the private preserve of a few people living in the largest cities. The Gramophone, the Pianola, and Broadcasting have changed all that. The Pianola has certain advantages over the Gramophone; for instance it allows you a say in the interpretation, and it gives you genuine piano tone. But the Gramophone has these great advantages over the Pianola—that it is cheaper and that it can reproduce voices, words, and the tone-colours of stringed and wind and percussion instruments; and though it costs rather more than Broadcasting it triumphs over that in one or two ways, for it allows you to choose your own concert times, programmes, and performers, and to repeat any item as many times as you wish. By means of the Gramophone people everywhere can enjoy the Queen's Hall Orchestra, or Chaliapin, or the London String Quartet, or Sammons, or Samuel, or Busoni. No other agency of musical reproduction for years to come is likely to reduce the popularity of the Gramophone. At all events it is as popular now as it ever was, and I am told by Gramophone dealers that if Broadcasting is affecting the sale of Records in any way, it is affecting them favourably, probably because it is spreading musical taste and awakening the desire to domesticate the most attractive of the works 'wirelessly' heard.

But people, I find, are crying out for a guide. The catalogues of the recording companies are enormous and heterogeneous. Moreover, some of the finest pieces of music included in them are at first found a little difficult of appreciation by the less experienced listener. So in this little book I have tried to be helpful. After days and weeks of careful testing of hundreds of Records by various makers, I have settled upon a choice of fifty, which I have here listed, arranged, so far as convenient, in historical order, explained and quoted in the form of music-type illustrations.

The Records mentioned in the present volume summarize in performance the various periods, styles and composers from Byrd to Beethoven; a second volume similarly summarizes the development of music from Beethoven to the present day. Probably further volumes will be added, which will abandon historical order, and catalogue and explain the best remaining Records of any period and any composer, including, of course, not merely fine Records previously omitted but also the best of those which may have appeared subsequently to the issue of the first two volumes.

This *First Book of the Gramophone Record*, though self-contained, may, if desired, be used as a companion to my *The Listener's History of Music, Vol. I—to Beethoven*, and the *Second Book*, when it appears, will offer a similar companionship to Vol. II of that History. I am not aware that there has previously appeared a History of Music illustrated by Gramophone Records, and I hope that many who, in the first instance, buy the present volume merely as a guide to the choice and use of Records may care to make such use more systematic and more educative by means of a parallel reading of the *Listener's History*, in which will be found a short account of the life of every composer represented in the fifty Records here recommended, and a description of the position he occupies in the story of the development of musical art.

To choose fifty Records out of thousands was an invidious task. No one principle has guided me. I have not chosen purely on grounds of (*a*) the good quality of the composition recorded, or (*b*) its good performance and good reproduction, or (*c*) its suitability as a type of the music of some composer or period. I have, instead, merged all these considerations, and chosen what, on a reasonable view, seemed to me to be nearest to meeting the lot of them. I am sure many readers will ask 'Why did you not include so-and-so?' But I believe that few, having become acquainted with what *is* included will protest against the inclusion of any item of it. In other words, in view of the limitation of number, there are inevitably sins of omission, but I hope there are few or no sins of commission.

One thing is certain (and it can be tested by any musician who cares to so much as glance through the Table of Contents)

—the man, woman, or child who has come to be well acquainted with the fifty Records I have described, or with a representative selection of them, has passed into intimacy with some of the world's greatest masterpieces.

It will be noted that, with the desire to be as practical as possible, I have in every case given the names of the manufacturers and the numbers and the prices of Records mentioned. But as to prices, observe that they are frequently changing—the tendency, happily, now being in a downward direction.

Certain gentle rudenesses towards the recording companies, to be found in the following pages, require perhaps a little softening here. It is encouraging to note that by the principal recording companies most of the older records of the classics are being gradually withdrawn and replaced, the 'cut' versions, several times disrespectfully alluded to in this book, giving place to complete versions. (In having complete versions substituted for cut versions, this book has in its Second Edition necessarily slightly outgrown its original total of fifty Records.) The first proofs of this book have, with great kindness, been read by the officials of every Record company mentioned. One of these, in a very friendly and 'sporting' spirit, wrote as follows concerning some of my remarks in the First Edition:

> 'We are amused at your remarks under Records Nos. — and —, but do you not realize that at the period these were made, our Company, alone among manufacturers, was developing this form of music because of a firm confidence in it, since completely justified? The issue of this Quartet on the small records (at a lower price than the large) was but part of a plan to interest the widest possible public in string quartet music. If, despite these facts, you still consider the terms of your criticism just, let it stand.'

I do still 'consider the terms of the criticism just', and therefore 'let it stand', but it is fair that this defence, which has a measure of reason in it, should likewise appear.

In addition to the co-operation of the Gramophone Company,

Ltd., the Columbia Graphophone Company, Ltd., and the Vocalion Gramophone Company, Ltd., members of whose staffs have, as before mentioned, very obligingly checked my work on the details already referred to, I have to thank the following firms both for permission to use musical illustrations from their publications, and for help in getting the references and prices of the printed music set down correctly: Messrs. Augener, Ltd., Messrs. J. and W. Chester, Ltd., Messrs. A. Durand & fils, The British and Continental Music Agency, Messrs. Goodwin & Tabb, Ltd., Messrs. Alfred Lengnick & Co., Messrs. Novello & Co., Ltd., Mr. Maurice Piena, Messrs. Stainer & Bell, Ltd., and Messrs. Joseph Williams, Ltd. I have also to thank Messrs. Alfred Imhof, of New Oxford Street, for help concerning certain Records; the Rev. Dr. E. H. Fellowes for very kindly checking the numerous and lengthy letterpress quotations from his *English Madrigal Composers*; Mr. W. R. Anderson, B.Mus., who has assisted me in the preparation of this book, and diligently read its proofs, and Mr. C. M. Crabtree, B.A., B.Mus., who has also participated in the latter service.

Since the First Edition appeared many fine Polydor and Parlophone Records have been issued, and some of these are now included in the scheme of the book.

A new and excellent 'Philharmonia' Edition of Miniature Scores is now available for some of the works included in this book (Hawkes & Son).

RECORD No. 1

Madrigals . . .	*All creatures now* . . .	Bennet
	In going to my naked bed . .	Edwards
	Fair Phyllis I saw . . .	Farmer

THE ENGLISH SINGERS.

John Bennet. *All creatures now are merry-minded.* (S.S.A.T.B.)

This is a five-voice Madrigal from *The Triumphs of Oriana.* The Madrigal was a choral form which flourished in Italy, England, and elsewhere at the end of the sixteenth century and beginning of the seventeenth. *The Triumphs of Oriana* was a collection of Madrigals written by various composers in honour of Queen Elizabeth, and edited by Thomas Morley. The title-page bears the date 1601, but the book actually appeared in 1603, just after the Queen's death. Under the name 'Oriana' all manner of virtues and graces are comprised, supposed to be those of the Queen. The book was a sort of national offering, twenty-three of the leading composers contributing one Madrigal apiece (John Milton, the poet's father, was amongst the twenty-three with a six-voice piece, *Fair Orian in the morn*). The words of Bennet's contribution to this collection are as follows:

All creatures now are merry merry minded,
The shepherds' daughters playing,
The nymphs are fa-la-laing.
Yond bugle was well winded.
At Orianaes presence each thing smileth,
The flowers themselves discover,
Birds over her do hover,
Music the time beguileth.
See where she comes with flowery garlands crowned
Queen of all queens renowned.
Then sang the shepherds and nymphs of Diana:
Long live fair Oriana.

A good deal of the beauty of this piece lies in the contrast between solid blocks of chords, as those with which the above extract opens, and quicker, running passages, in which the voices will often be heard to toss some little phrase from one to another. After several performances of the Record, and a little keen listening, there will be grasped a good deal of this latter treatment which had been at first missed, and the pleasure of listening will then be greatly increased.

Note the naïve, yet effective, little touch of realistic treatment at 'hover':

The ending 'Long live fair Oriana' is dignified, voice after voice taking up some point of imitation and the whole producing almost the effect of a piece of solid church music.

Richard Edwards. *In going to my naked bed.*

This composition is considerably earlier in date than any of the others mentioned in the present book. It anticipates the

Madrigal period proper, having been written not later than 1564, and possibly as early as 1550. Richard Edwards is known to be the author of the poem, and it is thought that he was also the composer of the music, inasmuch as he was a trained musician. And also his name appears attached to this piece, in what is known as the Mulliner MS.

The setting is for four voices (S.A.T.B.). The poem in full has five verses, of which but one is here set; in its completeness it appears in *The Paradise of Dainty Devices* (1578), and it has been reprinted by Dr. Fellowes in the edition of the Madrigal from which has been made the present Record. Dr. Fellowes also gives a description of the original manuscript of the composition, in the Mulliner MS. organ book; from this he has scored the piece—necessarily somewhat conjecturally, since the movement of the voices is not there clearly shown.

AMANTIUM IRAE AMORIS INTEGRATIO EST.

In going to my naked bed as one that would have slept,
I heard a wife sing to her child that long before had wept,
She sighèd sore and sung full sweet to bring the babe to rest,
That would not cease but criéd still in sucking at her breast.
She was full weary of her watch and grievèd with her child,
She rockèd it and rated it till that on her it smiled.
Then did she say: Now have I found this proverb true to prove
The falling out of faithful friends renewing is of love.

The music is exceedingly simple in harmony and dignified yet tender in feeling. Like the other choral pieces mentioned in this book it falls into a large number of short sections, each based upon some little phrase taken up in turn by the different voices.

John Farmer. *Fair Phyllis I saw sitting all alone.* (S.A.T.B.)

This is from *The First Set of English Madrigals to Foure Voices: Newly composed by IOHN Farmer, practicioner in the art of Musicque*, 1599.

Fair Phyllis I saw sitting all alone
    Feeding her flock near to the mountain side:
The shepherds knew not whither she was gone,
    But after her lover Amyntas hied,
Up and down he wandered whilst she was missing,
When he found her, oh they fell a kissing.

This is a very gentle, unpretentious, yet delicate Madrigal. Phyllis' loneliness is expressed at the outset by the words being given to the Soprano only. At the words 'The shepherds knew not', the voices take up the phrase one after another, almost as if expressive of wondering discussion as to Phyllis' whereabouts. Amyntas' wanderings 'up and down' are treated in a somewhat similar way; first one voice, then another, taking up the little phrase, so that you almost think you see Amyntas seeking, first in one place, then in another.

Small H.M.V. Record. E. 267, 4*s.* 6*d.*

Printed Music. All these pieces are sung as they appear in the standard edition of *The English Madrigal School*, edited by Rev. Dr. E. H. Fellowes (Stainer & Bell). The prices are as follows: *All Creatures*, 6*d.*; *In going*, 3*d.*; *Fair Phyllis*, 3*d.*

RECORD No. 2

Madrigals . . . . { *Lullaby, my sweet little baby* . . Byrd
{ *Sing we at pleasure* . . . . Weelkes

THE ENGLISH SINGERS.

William Byrd. *Lullaby, my sweet little baby.* (S.S.A.T.B.)

This is a five-voice Carol-Madrigal, from *Psalmes, Sonets, & songs of Sadnes and pietie, made into Musicque of five parts: whereof, some of them going abroade among divers, in untrue coppies are heere truely corrected, and th'other being Songs very rare and newly composed, are heere published, for the recreation of all such as delight in Musicke: By William Byrd, one of the Gent. of the Queenes Maiesties honorable Chappell.* (1588.)

Byrd dedicated this magnificent collection of thirty-five very varied pieces to the Lord Chancellor, Sir Christopher Hatton, 'incessantly beseeching our Lord to make your yeeres happie, and ende blessed', and he prefixed to it a persuasive document which cannot too often be reprinted:

¶ Reasons briefly set down by th'auctor, to perswade every one to learne to sing.

FIRST it is a knowledge easely taught, and quickly learned where there is a good Master, and an apt Scoller.

2. The exercise of singing is delightfull to Nature & good to preserve the health of Man.
3. It doth strengthen all the parts of the brest, & doth open the pipes.
4. It is a singuler good remedie for a stutting & stammering in the speech.
5. It is the best meanes to procure a perfect pronunciation & to make a good Orator.
6. It is the onely way to know where Nature hath bestowed the benefit of a good voyce . which guift is so rare, as there is not one among a thousand, that hath it: and in many, that excellent guift is lost, because they want Art to expresse Nature.
7. There is not any Musicke of Instruments whatsoever, comparable to

that which is made of the voyces of Men, where the voyces are good, and the same well sorted and ordered.

8. The better the voyce is, the meeter it is to honour and serve God there-with: and the voyce of man is chiefely to be imployed to that ende.

omnes spiritus laudet Dominum.

Since singing is so good a thing,
I wish all men would learne to sing.

The words of the Madrigal are as follows:

Lulla la lulla lulla lullaby,
My sweet little Baby, what meanest thou to cry.
Be still, my blessed babe, though cause thou hast to mourn,
Whose blood most innocent to shed the cruel king hath sworn;
And lo, alas, behold what slaughter he doth make,
Shedding the blood of infants all, sweet Saviour, for thy sake.
A King is born, they say, which King this king would kill.
O woe. and woeful heavy day, when wretches have their will!

But Byrd has set these words in two sections, or as we should say to-day two 'Movements', of which the present Record gives us only the first. The full words are reprinted above, to show the Christmas Carol nature of the work, but only the first two lines are here to be heard—the introductory cradle song, or croon, preceding the setting of the words of more definite import.

The rocking rhythm of the opening section will be noticed. The whole has a tinge of sadness well explained by the words that follow in the second movement.

Thomas Weelkes. *Sing we at pleasure.*

This is a five-voice (S.S.A.T.B.) Madrigal, from Weelkes's *Balletts and Madrigals to five voyces, with one to 6 voyces* (1598). In dedicating this volume to 'the right worshipful his Maister Edward Darcye Esquier', Weelkes wished him 'all heavenly ioyes whatsoeuer', and modestly lamented his own 'yeeres yet unripened, and this worke not a little hastened', and was careful not to 'promise any choice notes of Musicke'. Weelkes was at this time a young man of perhaps twenty-three, and this was his second published volume of choral pieces. The reference to 'his Maister' in the dedication indicates that he was in the domestic service, as musician, of the gentleman mentioned.

Sing we at pleasure
Content is our treasure.
Fa la la.
Sweet love shall keep the ground,
Whilst we his praises sound;
All shepherds in a ring
Shall dancing ever sing.
Fa la la.

The volume from which this comes was, as already noted, entitled *Balletts and Madrigals*, and this is one of the Balletts

—without being the less a Madrigal on that account. A Ballet is a Madrigal with a dance rhythm, and possibly some Ballets were both sung and danced. Whereas some of the Madrigals mentioned in this book are in places very free in their rhythms (so that the modern editor, in inserting the bars to which we are to-day accustomed and which we require, has had, in some cases, to place in them a varying number of beats), here, throughout, we have our steady three-in-a-bar.

Note too that on the whole the music is less 'contrapuntal', i.e. it often moves in solid blocks of harmony, though there are also from time to time phrases of melody taken up imitatively by one voice after another. As in some of the other madrigals, the voices cross a good deal, and until the piece is known, this obscures its lines to some extent.

The composition falls into two clearly defined halves, each ending with a *fa-la-* refrain and each repeated as it stands. It is a very cheerful piece of music, and might well be reserved for special occasions when a tonic is required, as for instance when payment of one's Income-tax becomes due, or when it rains on a Bank Holiday.

Small H.M.V. Record. E. 232, 4*s.* 6*d.*

Printed Music. Both pieces are sung from Dr. Fellowes' standard edition (Stainer & Bell)—*Lullaby*, 1st part 4*d.*, 2nd part 6*d.*, or complete 9*d.*; *Sing we*, 3*d.*

Just as this book goes to press for the Second Edition, H.M.V. issue a new recording of the English Singers in *Sing we* (E. 422, 4*s.* 6*d.*), which is almost perfect. On the reverse, this time, these Singers give us the folk-song *The Dark-eyed Sailor* arranged by Vaughan Williams, which will for many afford welcome variety from the Madrigals.

RECORD No. 3

Madrigals	*When David heard* . . .	Tomkins
	What is our Life? . . .	Gibbons

THE ENGLISH SINGERS.

Thomas Tomkins. *When David heard that Absalom was slain.*

This is a five-part (S.A.A.T.B.) piece from Tomkins' *Songs of 3, 4, 5, and 6 parts* (1622). There were two brothers, both Thomas Tomkins (confusing, but such was the occasional custom of the time). The elder lost his life in the 'Revenge', in its famous action under Sir Richard Greville; the younger became a pupil of Byrd, organist of Worcester Cathedral, and one of the organists of the Chapel Royal, and composed this and much other fine choral music.

When David heard that Absalom was slain
He went up to his Chamber over the Gate, and wept;
And thus he said:
O my son Absalom! my son, my son!
Would God I had died for thee,
O Absalom, my son, my son!

2 Samuel xviii. 33.

The music is solemn and affecting. It falls naturally into two sections. The first, of narration, ends, 'and thus he said', with a pause upon a half-close, or cadence of expectancy; then opens the second section, of lament, with poignant echoed and re-echoed cries, 'O my son'. Perhaps we may consider that a third section opens when, these cries ending for a moment, there comes the regret, 'Would God I had died for thee'. Then come the yearning cries again, and so, in hopeless despair, the piece ends.

(To prevent confusion it may be mentioned that there exist several other settings of these words, notably a fine one by Weelkes.)

Orlando Gibbons. *What is our Life?*

This is a five-voice setting (S.A.A.T.B.) of words usually attributed to Sir Walter Raleigh, and, from their style and thought, surely very probably his. Compare his 'For such is time', a poem of about the same length and with much the same thought, 'found in his Bible in the Gate House, at Westminster, 1618', and said to have been written the night before his execution. (The same statement is sometimes made about *What is our life?* but is obviously incorrect, since Gibbons' setting of this poem appeared six years before Raleigh's death.)

What is our life? a play of passion.
Our mirth the music of division.
Our mothers' wombs the tiring houses be,
Where we are dressed for this short Comedy.
Heaven the judicious sharp spectator is,
That sits and marks still who doth act amiss.
Our graves, that hide us from the searching sun,
Are like drawn curtains when the play is done.
Thus march we, playing, to our latest rest;
Only we die in earnest, that's no jest.

Walter Raleigh (1552–1618).

It is possible that this may at first, to some readers, be the least attractive of the madrigals mentioned in this book. Yet upon close familiarity it is quite likely to become one of the most attractive.

In order to attain full understanding and enjoyment, spend eightpence on the score, and play the Record several times, following the music closely though not laboriously. At each repetition fresh details will come to light until at last the structure will have become entirely clear. The best poetical description of choral counterpoint ever written (that of Milton, who had been reared in a contrapuntal atmosphere, since he was the son of a composer[1] who once received a gold medal and chain from a Polish prince, in reward for an 'In Nomine' in forty parts) may be looked upon as an apt description of such a piece as this:

> . . . notes, with many a winding bout
> Of linkèd sweetness long drawn out,
> With wanton heed and giddy cunning,
> The melting voice through mazes running,
> Untwisting all the chains that tie
> The hidden soul of harmony.

When the course of Gibbons' voices has been followed through their mazes, the chains that at present bind the soul of harmony are in sooth untwisted, and the soul of harmony has been freed. This process accomplished, begin to consider the composer's treatment of the words. As is usual in the

[1] See p. 1.

choral music of the period, he proceeds by taking up each verbal phrase and wedding it to some appropriate melodic phrase, given to the voices in turn, one voice often overlapping another as in the extract shown above.

The appropriateness of each musical phrase to the words it carries is marked. Note the solemnity of the opening question and answer.

This is developed for about twenty-five bars and then the next phrase is taken up:

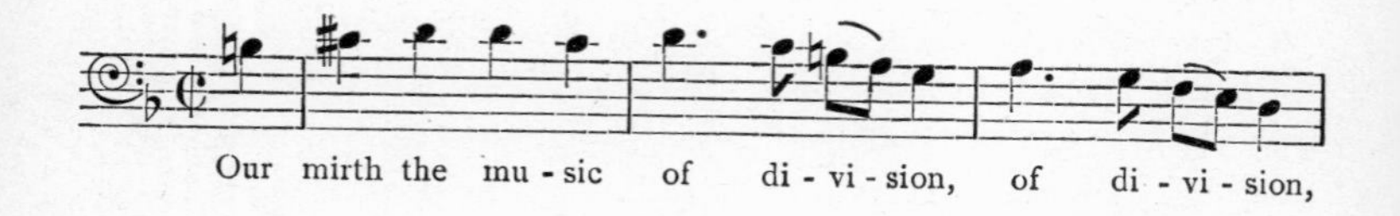

The change of feeling is apparent. Largely this is, of course, due to the quicker movement, the crotchet, instead of the minim, now becoming the unit. 'Division', in the seventeenth-century sense, meant a rapid passage—slow notes divided into quicker ones; the 'music of division' was therefore, often, and naturally, an expression of 'mirth'. Note that at the word 'division' the composer always drops into quaver movement.

The next phrases follow rapidly upon one another. Observe the severity of those set to 'the judicious sharp spectator', and 'sits and marks still who doth act amiss'.

Then opens a new section, with the end of the play and the thought of death as the drawing of the curtain—long-extended slow phrases:

There follows the thought of marching to music, with a steady rhythmic feeling throughout the passage, one voice after another taking up some firm little phrase. And so the piece draws to its end.

Large H.M.V. Record. D. 663, 6*s*. 6*d*.

Printed Music. In Fellowes' 'English Madrigal School' edition (Stainer & Bell). Each piece costs 8*d*.

RECORD No. 4

Madrigals . . . { *Stay, Corydon, thou swain* . . . . Wilbye
{ *Cupid, in a Bed of Roses* . . . Bateson

THE ENGLISH SINGERS.

John Wilbye. *Stay, Corydon, thou swain.*

This is a six-voice Madrigal (S.S.A.T.T.B.), first published in 1609 in Wilbye's *The Second Set of Madrigales to* 3, 4, 5, *and* 6 *parts apt both for Voyals and Voyces.* By 'Voyals' understand Viols (the precursors of our present Violin family); it was not unusual at this date, when no large amount of music existed specially written for stringed instruments, to make instrumental use of choral music in the way suggested here.

Stay, Corydon, thou swain,
Talk not so soon of dying.
What though thy heart be slain?
What though thy love be flying?
She threatens thee but dares not strike,
Thy Nymph is light and shadow-like:
For if thou follow her, she'll fly from thee,
But if thou fly from her, she'll follow thee.

This is a rather steady-going Madrigal, which gains upon one's affections as one becomes more acquainted with it.

Note how the composer has everywhere accepted the suggestion of the words. 'Stay' in the opening (see above) set to long-held notes; 'flying' to the first quavers we have yet heard; 'she threatens thee' to a truculent little phrase:

'Thy Nymph is light and shadow-like' to a delicate, quickly moving phrase; 'For if thou follow her' to a passage in which the voices follow closely on one another's heels, in a cleverly devised piece of close imitation or 'canon'.

Bateson. *Cupid, in a Bed of Roses.*

This is a six-voice (S.S.A.T.T.B.) Madrigal from *The Second Set of Madrigales to* 3, 4, 5 *and* 6 parts: *Apt for Viols and Voyces. Newly composed by Thomas Bateson, Batcheler of Musicke, Organist, and Master of the Children of the Cathedrall Church of the Blessed Trinitie, Dublin, in the Realme of Ireland.* (1618.) It was usual at this period to dedicate a volume of Madrigals or of poetry to some nobleman, and Bateson dedicated these to Lord Chichester, the Lord High Treasurer of Ireland of the day: *Because they were solely entended for your Honors private recreation, after your tedious imployments in the affayres of the common-wealth, being then his Majesties most worthy Deputy, and swaying the sword and scepter of authority amongst us, in this kingdome of Ireland.*

(*The first portion.*)

Cupid, in a bed of roses
Sleeping, chanced to be stung
Of a bee that lay among
The flowers where he himself reposes.

And thus to his mother, weeping,
Told that he this wound did take
Of a little wingèd snake,
As he lay securely sleeping.

(*The second portion.*)

Cytherea, smiling, said
That if so great sorrow spring
From a silly bee's weak sting,
As should make thee thus dismayed,
What anguish feel they, think'st thou, and what pain,
Whom thy empoisoned arrows cause complain?

These words are a translation of an Ode of Anacreon. They are set as what we may call a Two-Movement Madrigal, Movement I recounting Cupid's mischance, and Movement II his mother's very pertinent reply.

Part I begins:

Note the dreamy drawn-out expression of 'sleeping', the plaintive 'weeping', and so on.

Part II begins:

The pleasant little sound-painting devices continue, e.g. 'smiling', 'anguish', &c. At 'whom thy empoisoned arrows cause complain' there is a suggestion of a little succession of the tiny darts flying here and there through the air, as Cupid twangs his bow.

The whole piece proceeds, as do so many of these Madrigals, in a series of short passages, each, as a rule, taking up some fresh little pointed phrase, suitable to the new verbal phrase, and treating it in a sort of game-of-ball fashion, i. e. passing it rapidly from one member of the party to another, and so in a few seconds round the whole set of performers.

Small H.M.V. Record. E. 260, 4*s*. 6*d.*

Printed Music. Again the edition used is Fellowes' *The English Madrigal School* (Stainer & Bell). *Stay, Corydon* costs 8*d.*, the two parts of *Cupid* 4*d.* and 6*d.* respectively.

RECORD No. 5

Harpsichord Solos . . . { *Galliard* . . . . . John Bull
{ *Allemande* . . . . Bach

MRS. VIOLET GORDON WOODHOUSE.

Bull. *Galliard.*

There is little to be said about this piece. Bull (1562–1628) was a famous player of the Virginals and the Organ (for a few particulars of his adventurous life, see *The Listener's History of Music*, Vol. I, page 46), and his keyboard music well represents the effort the English composers were making, at the turn of the sixteenth–seventeenth centuries, to bring into existence forms and styles of composition, and a technique of performance which should fully exploit the powers of the domestic keyboard instrument of the day, the Virginals.

A Galliard is an old dance form—the 'nimble Galliard' of Shakespeare (*Henry V*, I. ii): 'What is thy excellence in a Galliard, Knight?' asks Sir Toby of Sir Andrew, in *Twelfth Night* (I. iii).

The attempts of the Elizabethan virginalists to find suitable forms for Virginal music took three main lines—(1) They imitated choral music, in 'Fantazias' and incipient Fugues, or (2) They imitated and embellished the dance forms, e.g. in a dignified Pavan followed by a 'nimble Galliard' (i.e. a rudimentary form of 'Suite', leading in the direction of the Sonata and Symphony of our own day), or (3) They took some popular tune and used it as the basis for a string of Variations.

This Galliard of Bull's shows the (not infrequent) combination of two of these ideas. It is a piece in dance style, divided into two parts, each of them followed by a variation.

The first part opens thus:

It is immediately followed by a simple Variation in quicker notes, and Air and Variation are then repeated.

The second part opens thus:

It also is immediately followed by a variation, and then air and variation are, as before, repeated. This ends the piece.

This Galliard is found in the great manuscript collection of keyboard music preserved in the Fitzwilliam Library at Cambridge, being known under the erroneous description of *Queen Elizabeth's Virginal Book*, but now always called *The Fitzwilliam Virginal Book.* This book has come down the ages as a record of the efforts and achievements of the English musicians of its time; the first mention of it is as one of the volumes in the library of Dr. Pepusch, at the sale of which, in 1762, it fetched but ten guineas, which is about the same one has to pay to-day for a second-hand copy of the Breitkopf and Härtel reprint of 1899, which is unfortunately scarce, and difficult to obtain. It ought to be a point of national honour to publish both a facsimile edition and an edition in modern notation, and to keep these in print.

The Galliard of this period may to some at first sound a little confused and uninteresting. Listen to it, however, several times, in a quiet spirit, and it will be found to make its effect. The Fitzwilliam version from which the above extracts are taken differs in a few notes from the version played by Mrs. Gordon Woodhouse, who has evidently either had access to some other manuscript copy, or has herself transcribed the piece from the Fitzwilliam Book, interpreting its notation a little differently from Messrs. Fuller Maitland and Barclay Squire, the editors of the Breitkopf and Härtel volumes.

Bach. *Allemande from First Partita.*

Bach wrote three famous sets of Keyboard Suites:

The Six 'French Suites'.

The Six 'Partitas' sometimes called 'German Suites'.

The Six 'English Suites'.

(The 'French Suites', it has been conjectured, were so called as being written in the lighter, clearer, French style; the 'English Suites' have been so called from a misconception, of which a full account can be seen in Parry's *John Sebastian Bach*, pages 462–3; the 'Partitas' have been called 'German Suites' simply by analogy with the 'French' and 'English' Suites. The 'French Suites' are, as a rule, the lightest and gayest, and the 'English Suites' the most solid, thoughtful, and highly developed.)

The First Partita (in B flat), from which this Allemande comes, consists of seven 'movements' as follows:

Prelude,
Allemande,
Courante,
Sarabande,
Minuet I,
Minuet II,
Gigue.

This is much the normal scheme of a Bach suite.

An *Allemande* was a movement in $\frac{4}{4}$ time, originally a dance in moderate *tempo*, and its first phrase generally opened with a short unaccented note (many of the following phrases necessarily therefore doing the same). It consisted of two sections, each repeated (i.e. it was in 'Binary Form').

Listening to this Record, the FIRST SECTION will be found to open with the very lively running *arpeggio* passages given above, and to continue in this style until, at the twelfth bar, in the right-hand part, a more definite and expressive melody creeps in (it is smoother in motion, and hence well contrasted with the preceding, arpeggiated, theme):

Shortly after this the First Section comes to an end (in the key of the Dominant, i.e. it begins in B flat and ends in F).

The First Section is then repeated.

The SECOND SECTION is constructed very much like the First. The same two themes appear. This section begins in the key in which the previous section left off (i. e. F) and ends in the key in which the previous section began (i. e. B flat); it has more passing modulations, or changes of key, than the first section (note the fine effect of contrast Bach gets by using the minor keys in the earlier half of this Second Section; this makes the return to the major, at the end, very effective also), and is a little extended, at the end, in order that the piece as a whole may have a very definite and effective conclusion.

This is an excellent specimen of Bach's livelier keyboard style. Parry (*John Sebastian Bach*, page 459) says:

'It is the most graceful and fluent of all Bach's numerous movements of the kind [i. e. his Allemandes], but so slight as to have an almost evanescent delicacy, and in that quality shows very marked contrast to the weighty Allemandes in the English Suites.'

Small H.M.V. Record. E. 275, 4*s.* 6*d.*

Printed Music. Bull, *Galliard*, not to be obtained except in the expensive publication mentioned in the text above; where it will be found on page 249 of Vol. II.

Bach, *Allemande*. This Record offers an example of the ignorantly ambiguous labelling which is still common amongst the Gramophone companies. It runs:

ALLEMANDE—SECOND MOVEMENT
(1st Partita in B♭).

By this is meant

ALLEMANDE
(2nd movement of 1st Partita, in B♭).

It can be found in any edition of the Partitas, e. g. 1st vol. of the edition in 2 vols., Augener's edition, No. 7981 a (each vol. 2*s.* 8*d.*).

RECORD No. 6

Song . . . *Arise, ye subterranean winds!* . . . Purcell
(From *The Tempest.*)
NORMAN ALLIN.
(With Orchestra.)

Purcell. *Arise, ye subterranean winds.*

Arise, ye subterranean winds,
More to distract their guilty minds.
Arise, ye winds whose rapid force can make
All but the fix'd and solid centre shake;
Come drive these wretches to that part o' th' Isle
Where nature never yet did smile.
Come fogs and damps, whirlwinds and earthquakes there,
There let them howl and languish in despair.
Rise and obey the pow'rful prince o' th' air.

(THOMAS SHADWELL.)

This song comes from a so-called 'opera' (really a play with a good deal of incidental music), by Shadwell, based upon Shakespeare. The opera was produced in 1673, at Dorset Gardens theatre, and is thus described by John Downes, in his *Roscius Anglicanus*:

'*The Tempest*, or *The Enchanted Island*, made into an opera by Mr. Shadwell, having all new in it; as Scenes, Machines; particularly one scene painted with myriads of *Ariel* Spirits; and another flying away with a Table Furnish't out with Fruits, Sweet Meats, and all sorts of Viands; just when Duke Trinculo and his companions were going to Dinner; all things perform'd in it so Admirably well, that not any succeeding opera got more money.'

The music in the early performances of this opera was by Matthew Locke and others, Purcell's being, apparently, contributed on the occasion of a later performance.

The general position of this song in the play is pretty obvious. It is sung by a devil who takes part in the punishment of Antonio, Alonzo, and Gonzalo.

The music is a magnificent example of what we usually consider the florid Handelian style. But Handel was only ten years of age when Purcell died, and the resemblance is accounted for partly by the fact that Handel and Purcell, though their active working lives are separated by some years [1] belong to the same general period in the development of music, and partly, no doubt, by the fact that Handel's best work was done after he had settled in England and become acquainted with Purcell's music, which, at the period of his arrival here (1710) was the most popular in use in this country.

Notice how descriptive Purcell tries to be. The opening phrase, already quoted, is an example. Here are some others:

[1] Purcell, 1658 (or 1659)–1695; Handel, 1685–1759.

and lan - - - - - - - - guish in des-pair.

In Purcell's days the Orchestra was still in an embryonic state. According to existing manuscripts of this Song the accompaniment would be played by a body of Strings, with a Harpsichordist supplying a general background. In the performance recorded a fuller modern Orchestra is used—with discretion, and with excellent effect, on the whole, though there are a few notes not quite 'in the picture', e.g. immediately following my last musical quotation. One could also find a few imperfections in performance, both vocal and instrumental; but on the whole this is a Record in which every one can revel.

Four bars of the little instrumental interlude following the singer's first entry have been omitted in making this Record.

On the reverse is J. W. Elliott's once popular *Song of Hybrias the Cretan*—a song of the 'I'm a brave fellow' type, rather aggressive, perhaps, but well-meaning.

Large Columbia Record. L. 1414, 6*s.* 6*d.*

Printed Music. All the *Tempest* music will be found (full score) in the Purcell Society's Edition, vol. xix (Novello, 25*s.*). This particular Song, with pianoforte accompaniment, is published in various editions (e.g. Novello, 1*s.* 6*d.*).

RECORD No. 7

Pianoforte Solos . .	*Prelude*	Purcell
	Sarabande	,,
	Minuets	,,
	(from Harpsichord Suites).	

IRENE SCHARRER.

Purcell. *Prelude from Fifth Suite for Harpsichord.*

This exhilarating trifle requires little description. It is a sort of incipient Fugue, usually in two parts, but towards the end sometimes in three, or even four.

Beginning as shown above, with the 'Subject' in the Treble and the 'Answer' in the Bass, it comes, after much further responsive treatment of this kind, to a sort of 'half-way house' in the Dominant key (i. e. beginning in Key C it here reaches Key G). Then it returns to the original key, and the Subject enters in the Bass and is then taken up in the Treble (reversing the opening procedure).

Thence the piece proceeds very merrily to the end. (This is thus a sort of Fugue in Binary Form, and in both form and spirit resembles, in its very simple way, the Gigue as treated by Bach in his Suites.)

Purcell. *Sarabande from Suite II.*

The Sarabande was a slow and stately dance in triple time. Shakespeare (*Much Ado*, II. i) speaks of a 'wedding mannerly-modest as a measure, full of state and ancientry', and this is, no doubt, the sort of 'measure' he had in mind.

Like much of the instrumental music of the Purcell-Bach-Handel period, the Sarabande was in Binary Form, i.e. it fell into two sections, with a Cadence in the middle.

In this piece the first section begins, as shown above, in the key of G minor. Then, at Bar 8 this section ends with a 'Full

Close', or 'Perfect Cadence' in the Relative Major key (i.e. B flat major).

Then the Second Section begins, working its way back, after a little varied modulation, in another eight bars, to the original key.

The last four bars are then repeated, and so ends the Second Section.

Properly each of the two sections should be played twice, but in the performance recorded only the Second Section has been so treated.

It may be of some little interest to note that the four Movements of this Suite are (named in order) Prelude, Almand, Corant, and Saraband, thus showing already accepted very much the Bach sequence of pieces (e.g. see p. 21).

Purcell. *Minuets from Suites I and VIII.*

Minuet from Suite I.

Minuet from Suite VIII.

Two Minuet Movements from different Suites have here been put into the same key, and alternated as follows:

Minuet from Suite I,
" " " VIII (transposed into Key C),
" " " I.

The arrangement is not unsuitable, but it would have been a more artistic thing, instead of making up this Record with Movements from various Suites, to have given one Suite in full.

The two Minuets begin as shown above. Each of them is in Binary Form, with (in this performance) only its first half repeated.

In the music several signs appear above the notes (such as are, by the way, not all known to the keyboard players of to-day). It will be borne in mind that the keyboard music of this period was written not for the modern Pianoforte but for the Harpsichord, an instrument without the sustaining power of the Pianoforte. It was a natural thing, therefore (and especially so in a slow movement), to prolong the sound of a note by adorning or 'ornamenting' it. In some cases, too, a note of importance was given an additional ictus, by being introduced by a rapid little ornament (see first note in Saraband above). Cases of both uses will be found in this piece. In playing such music upon the Pianoforte some of these ornaments are sometimes omitted.

Furthermore, it is arguable that some of these pieces gain by judicious filling-up when they are to be played on the Pianoforte. The pieces here recorded are, however, 'adapted' to a regrettable degree, and the Record is included in this book because there are no better examples of Purcell's Keyboard Music at present available.

Large H.M.V. Record. D. 622, 6*s*. 6*d*.

(On the reverse Sinding's *Rustle of Spring* played by the same artist.)

Printed Music. The first piece on this record, vaguely entitled, on the label, *Toccata Prelude* (*from a Suite for Harpsichord*), is the Prelude from Suite V (vol. i of the 4 vols. of Purcell's Harpsichord Music, edited by W. Barclay Squire, and published by Chester at 3*s*. per vol.). The other pieces on the record are correctly described on the label, the *Sarabande* being from Suite II (vol. i, collection just mentioned), and the Minuets respectively from Suite I (vol. i) and Suite VIII (vol. ii). The label bears the note 'transcribed by A. M. Henderson' (which indicates that the player has used the volume *Early Classic Masters*, Bayley & Ferguson, 2*s*. 6*d*.).

RECORD No. 8

The Golden Sonata . . . . Purcell
ISOLDE MENGES, WILLIAM PRIMROSE, AND H. Y. TEMPLEMAN.

Purcell. *The Golden Sonata.*

This is one of 'TEN SONATA'S in FOUR PARTS. Compos'd by the LATE MR. HENRY PURCELL. *London*, Printed by *J. Heptinstall*, for *Frances Purcell*, Executrix of the Author; And are to be sold by *B. Aylmer* at the Three Pigeons against the Royal Exchange, *W. Henchman* in *Westminster-Hall*, and *Henry Playford* at his Shop in the *Temple-Change*, *Fleet-street.* 1697.'

As this title-page tells us, they were first published by Purcell's wife, Frances, two years after the Composer's death. She dedicated them to the Lady Rhodia Cavendish, being 'desirous that it might not want the Patronage of our Sex'. Frances Purcell tells us that the Lady Cavendish had made 'wonderfull Progress . . . in all Ingenuous Accomplishments, and particularly in this of Musick', and that 'the dear Author of these Compositions . . . had the Honour to be Your Master'.

Note that *The Golden Sonata* is only one among ten such pieces. Indeed it is one among twenty-two, for Purcell also wrote Twelve Sonatas 'in Three Parts' (really just as much in four as the others, since both sets are for three Stringed Instruments, plus one Keyboard Instrument). And though this 'Golden' Sonata is the most popular, and is fairly well known as one of the finest pieces of Chamber Music in existence, it is by no means the only good one, perhaps not even the best. Any violinist would find it well worth while to look through the other twenty-one.

The Four Parts are for two Violins, a 'Cello, and the Keyboard Instrument. (In making this Record the 'Cello part has been omitted. This is a less serious loss than might be supposed, since the 'Cello does little more than double the bass of the Keyboard part.)

Readers will find it interesting to compare this early Sonata with the type afterwards evolved in the Haydn-Mozart-Beethoven period. (See 'Sonata' and 'Sonata-Form' in Glossary.)

This piece consists of five Movements, as follows:

Slow, in a broad style,
Slow,
Quick,
Very Slow and Solemn,
Quick.

Movement I is a massive preludial Movement, fashioned largely out of the opening bars, and especially out of the figure (*a*) first heard in the bass:

Note that at the third bar the Violins play that bass theme 'in augmentation' (in this case, half as slow again) and then take it up at its original speed.

Movement II consists entirely of 'suspensions' (i.e. progressions in which some notes are held up while others move) and of expressive, gliding, chromatic harmonies.

Movement III is a lively 'Canzona', or piece in fugal style. The Subject is here given out by First Violin:

It is immediately answered by the Second Violin, then, in the bass, by the Keyboard. In the course of this Movement there is much deliciously dainty imitation and interlacing of the two Violins.

Movement IV is a short, serious-minded interlude. Note at the opening Purcell's characteristic free use of a phrase *two-and-a-half* bars long.

Movement V is a very gay, dance-like piece. It is another fugal piece, and the Subject:

is again given out by First Violin, immediately answered by Second, and then by the bass. When the bass enters, the First Violin has a definite Countersubject, which, in fact, plays an important part in the Movement.

Again there is delightful interplay of the Violins.

In a piece of Chamber Music of this period the keyboard part was usually a mere line of bass notes, with some figures indicating the chords out of which the harpsichordist or organist was extemporaneously to erect an accompaniment. Necessarily, then, the keyboard part as seen in our modern editions of such a piece is, save for its bass line and the choice of harmonies, the work of some modern musician.

Large H.M.V. Record. D. 889, 6*s.* 6*d.*

Printed Music. All the Ten Sonatas were edited by Sir Charles Stanford (Purcell Society, Novello, 30*s.*). The Twelve Sonatas are also published for the Purcell Society. (Separate Violin Parts are not published.)

The *Golden Sonata* has been edited separately by G. Jensen (Augener, 3*s.*), and this is the edition here recorded. The keyboard part is good, though not as interesting as Stanford's arrangement, which is probably very like what a first-rate harpsichordist of the day would have played.

RECORD No. 9

Harpsichord Pieces . .	*Gavotte*	Purcell
	Prelude	Bach
	L'Arlequin	Couperin
	Tambourin	Rameau

MRS. GORDON WOODHOUSE.

Purcell. *Gavotte.*

The Gavotte was a dance form of French origin in $\frac{2}{2}$ or $\frac{4}{4}$ time, in regular 2-bar phrases, all of which began half-way through the bar (a Bourrée was a very similar piece, but its phrases began at three-quarters-way through the bar).

This particular very graceful Gavotte is in a simple sort of Rondo form, i.e. it begins with a main tune that recurs—

Main Tune (8 bars),
Another Tune (8 bars),
Main Tune (as before),
Still another Tune (8 bars),
Main Tune (slightly varied).

Mr. Barclay Squire, in editing Purcell's Harpsichord Music for the Purcell Society, included this Gavotte as plausibly Purcell's—'The Gavotte has no composer's name, but as it occurs in the midst of a set of pieces by Purcell, there can be but little doubt that it is also by him.' (The source of this Gavotte and the other pieces mentioned was a manuscript, at that time belonging to Dr. Cummings. Whoever was the composer, it is a charmingly fresh little piece. The present writer admits that to him it does not sound quite like Purcell.)

Bach. *Prelude in E flat.*

This is a delicate little piece, a good deal of which is similar in style to the first Prelude of the '48' (see p. 53), that is, it is based upon an arpeggio treatment of a series of simple but beautifully progressing chords.

Then in the middle there comes a passage of a different kind, with a little contrapuntal imitation, whilst at the end there is once more a passing touch of the opening style.

François Couperin. *L'Arlequin.*

A dainty, musical-boxy little piece, almost entirely constructed out of the *motif* shown above.

It is in Simple Binary Form, with a short First Part and a longer Second Part, each of them repeated.

Jean-Philippe Rameau. *Tambourin.*

A Tambourin is an old French form, of which Rameau's contemporary, Jean-Jacques Rousseau, in his *Dictionary of Music*, gives the following definition:

'**Tambourin.** A kind of dance very much in fashion nowadays in the French theatre. Its tune is very gay, and in a quick duple time. It ought to be skipping and well-cadenced, in imitation of the flute of Provençals; and the bass ought to strike again and again the same note, in imitation of the *Tambourin* or galoubé, with which the fife player generally accompanied himself.'

Apparently Rousseau makes a slip here, since the Provençal flute and the Galoubé (or Galoubet) are the same instrument, and the Tambourin, so far from being the same as the Galoubé, is a sort of long, narrow drum.

Practically the Provençal Galoubet and Tambourin were the same as the old English Pipe and Tabor, and just as the latter were played simultaneously by the one performer, so were the former.

Readers of Daudet's *Trente ans de Paris* will remember his sketch of a Provençal *Tambourinaire* who had been sent to him by Mistral, and will probably have seen some illustrations of him, with his pipe and his drum. And readers of the same author's delightful novel, *Numa Roumestan*, will require no description of the instruments and their music (the popular Nelson edition of this book, in the original French, has a frontispiece showing a performance).

The extract given above shows something of the harmonic structure of the piece. The low left-hand E continues through the piece, and, except for a few bars in the middle, the B continues with it. These persistent bass notes represent, of course, the drum, as the treble melody represents the fife.

Constructionally the problem of the piece is to get enough variety whilst tethered all the time to one bass note. Rameau has been very clever in doing this. His scheme is roughly:

(*a*) Tune I (8 bars, beginning as above).

(*b*) Tune II (8 bars, similar to I, but lying at a higher pitch).

(*c*) Tune I (as before).
(*d*) Tune III (beginning in a more modulatory fashion, and also 'developing' two little *motifs* of the Tune I).
(*e*) Tune I (as before).
(*f*) Tune IV (10 bars, merging, in the midst of a running passage, imperceptibly into the next section).
(*g*) Tune I (altered at its opening, and embellished with more runs).

It may seem that the description of this little piece has been rather laboured, but it illustrates very admirably principles that are found in all instrumental music, and that, fundamental as they are, are overlooked by many people who have not had a technical musical training.

One of these principles is economy of material. Note that this whole piece is made out of material shown in the extract above. The closest listening will hardly discover any bar in the piece which is not either constructed out of one of the four little *motifs* marked (1), (2), (3), (4) in the extract given, or out of some slight 'development' of one of these *motifs*.

Observe, by the way, in Section III, the harmonic variety that is skilfully introduced into the first four bars, the 'pedal' E still standing throughout; the upper part here is a development of *motif* (3). Then notice the little touch of contrapuntal variety in the following four bars, the *motif* (1) being given alternately to right hand and left hand.

This piece of over sixty bars long is entirely made out of four tiny half-bar *motifs*, over one standing bass note.

The principle of a standing bass, or 'Pedal', which is constantly made use of in music to-day, and which, indeed, extended in its application, accounts for a good deal of our most violently 'modern' harmony, probably had a 'folk' origin in the use of such instruments as the pipe with its tabor, or the bagpipe and its drone.

Large H.M.V. Record. D. 490, 6*s.* 6*d.*

Printed Music. Purcell, *Gavotte.* In vol. vi of the Purcell Society publications, p. 50 (Novello, 25*s.*). Not at present included in any other Purcell collection. (Mrs. Gordon Woodhouse appears to have used some old manuscript version differing slightly from the printed one.)

Couperin, *Arlequin.* Louis Diémer's standard edition in 4 vols. (Durand, Paris), vol. iv, p. 52 (there called 'Arlequin*e*'). Brahms-Chrysander edition (Augener, 4 books, each 6*s.*); in vol. iv.

Rameau, *Tambourin.* This may be found on p. 32 of Saint-Saëns' standard edition of Rameau's Harpsichord Works (1 vol., Durand, Paris, 2 francs). It is also published separately by Augener, price 9*d.*

Bach, *Prelude.* Only to be had in the great Bachgesellschaft edition (vol. xxxvii, part ii, Supplement ii, p. 234).

RECORD No. 10

Harpsichord Solos	*Prelude from 3rd English Suite*[1] . .	Bach
	The Harmonious Blacksmith . . .	Handel

MRS. GORDON WOODHOUSE.

Bach. *Prelude from Third English Suite.*

This attractive movement is constructed of a number of tiny *motifs* (mostly a bar in length), which are almost all shown in the extract given above. If that extract be observed closely it will be found to be made up of four such *motifs*; and out of these and a few others closely related to them is made the whole piece.

Little more than that need be told to the ordinary listener, but if any reader wishes to observe in detail how Bach has made up his long piece from small material the following may help him.

[1] Called 1st English Suite on label.

It is in short sections as follows:

Section I (bars 1–21). Begins in G minor and comes to half-close in that key.

Section II (bars 22–33). Modulates a good deal and comes to full-close in G minor.

Section III (bars 33–67, a longer section). Comes to a full-close in the key of B flat major. In this section a good deal is made of three new *motifs*, which are seen in the following passage:

Section IV (bars 67–87). Reproduces Section I, but in the key of B flat major (i.e. in the Tonic Major).

Section V (bars 88–99). Corresponds to Section II, but with some changes in the upper parts.

Section VI (bars 99–125). A longish section working towards and ending with a full-close in D minor (=Dominant key).

Section VII (bars 125–160). Corresponds to the long Section III, transposed, but the course of its modulations is somewhat changed, and it ends in Key E flat major.

Section VIII (bars 160–end). A brilliant final section, using the old material, and enforcing the main key of the piece, G minor.

All that looks very dry, and so it is to anybody who does not take an interest in musical construction. To one who does, however, the process of effectively making a four or five minutes' piece out of four or five seconds' worth of material will always seem worth study. And having made his study he will forget all about it, yet find that he now enjoys the piece better, and not, as some might expect, worse. for having taken it to bits and put it together again.

Handel. *The Harmonious Blacksmith.*[1]

This should properly be called 'Air and Variations from the Fifth Harpsichord Suite'. (As played by Mrs. Woodhouse the Air shown above is embellished in the manner of the period. See p. 29.)

The Suites were published in 1720. Nearly a century later this movement got its name in the way thus described by the late Dr. Cummings in his *Handel, The Duke of Chandos, The Harmonious Blacksmith* ('Musical News' Office, 1915):

'At the beginning of the nineteenth century there was in the city of Bath a firm of music-sellers, J. & W. Lintern. The son William had in youth been apprenticed to a blacksmith, but possessed of natural musical gifts, he assiduously cultivated them, and attained to considerable facility as a pianist. He therefore abandoned his early occupation and adopted music as a profession. He frequently played for the delectation of his father and friends, and was nicknamed by them "the harmonious blacksmith". The favourite piece of the Lintern circle was the Air with Variations from Handel's Fifth Suite, copies of which were frequently asked for. Lintern, with an eye to business, therefore determined to publish it, and very sagaciously gave the piece the title which would identify it with his own personality. . . . The precise date of Lintern's

[1] I have rebarred this, the original barring (which runs right through the piece) being, in my judgement, palpably wrong.

publication is not known, but Bath was a fashionable resort and Handel's Air with its romantic title soon became a popular piece in all musical circles.'

In 1835 a letter appeared in *The Times* from an anonymous correspondent, probably the possessor of a gift of humour.

'An inquiry was made through the medium of a late musical periodical if any information could be given by its correspondents concerning the origin of Handel's charming melody of "The Harmonious Blacksmith" and why it was so called. No reply seems to have reached the Editor (for we looked for it in vain). The following traditionary particulars may not be unacceptable:

"When Handel was at Canons, the far-famed residence of the magnificent Duke of Chandos, near Edgware, he was one day overtaken in his walks by a heavy shower of rain; the great composer took shelter under a blacksmith's shop by the roadside, where its laborious occupant was beating the iron on the anvil, and singing at his work. The varying sounds of the falling hammer on the metal mingled with the rude tones of the man's voice, and entered into the very soul of the attentive listener. He carried home with him the feelings, the character, the inspiration of an idea admirable alike for the beauty and simplicity of its development, and gave us for a 'rich legacy' the notation of the few touching phrases which we have received under the name (bestowed upon it by himself) of *The Harmonious Blacksmith*, an effusion the sweetness of which has drawn tears from many a gentle eye, and equally impressed with its melodious power the minds of the most refined musicians of Europe for now nearly a hundred years; a composition indeed replete

With image, music, sentiment and thought
Never to die".'

And so the story was floated—'never to die'. The anvil upon which the blacksmith hammered as he sang to Handel has been sold by auction as a precious relic (where is it now, by the way?), and nothing that can be written in the press will stir the Vicar and Churchwardens to remove or amend the tasteful tombstone 'Erected by Subscription', to 'William Powell, The Harmonious Blacksmith' (with its two notes in musical notation, supposed to represent the anvil's accompaniment to the blacksmith's tune) whose record begins *In memory of* but should begin *Here Lies*.[1]

[1] The more so since it goes on to speak of Handel as 'Organist of the Church', which he never was, though he was organist of the Duke of Chandos's private chapel in the park adjoining.

The short Air out of which this long piece is constructed itself grows out of one little *motif* (the two notes with which it opens), which, embellished, or inverted, or extended, make up its whole structure. This is worthy of mention, as there must be some readers who have not had their attention drawn to the organic nature of any good tune.

The Variations are extremely unsophisticated.

I *a*. Right-hand part divided up into 'broken-chord' semiquavers.

I *b*. Left-hand part similarly treated.

II *a*. Right-hand part broken up into rather smaller fractions still—triplet semiquavers.

II *b*. Left-hand similarly treated.

III. Grand finale, with sometimes the right-hand and sometimes the left-hand part broken into the still smaller fractions of demisemiquavers—in rapid scale rushes, upward or downward.

Thus, the general scheme of the piece is one of growing excitement through ever-increasing velocity. Its beautiful theme and its simplicity of effect have made it popular with listeners, and the fact that it is a great deal less difficult than it sounds has long been counted a virtue in it by the amateur pianist.

Large H.M.V. Record. D. 645, 6*s*. 6*d*.

Printed Music. The Bach piece is labelled on the Record 'First English Suite, 1st movement'; it should read '*Third* English Suite (in G minor), 1st Movement'. The *English Suites* can be got in the Augener edition (Nos. 8017 a, b), in 2 vols., each 2*s*. 6*d*. The Suite in question is in vol. i.

The Harmonious Blacksmith (so called) will be found in Suite V, of which it is the last movement. The Handel Suites are published in various editions, as for instance, in the Peters edition in 2 vols. (each 4*s*.), the piece in question being found in vol. i. Under the title *The Harmonious Blacksmith* it can be separately purchased in various editions at any music shop.

Orchestral Suite . *Brandenburg Concerto in G, No. 3* . . . Bach

ORCHESTRA OF THE STATE OPERA HOUSE, BERLIN.
(Conducted by Georg Hoeberg.)
or
ROYAL ALBERT HALL ORCHESTRA.
(Conducted by Eugene Goossens.)

Bach. *Brandenburg Concerto in G, No. 3.*

The six Brandenburg Concertos were made for a Count of Brandenburg, a great lover of music who was making a collection of concertos by contemporary composers for his private band to perform. When the Count died and his property had to be valued, the Bach works were, in the inventory, lumped together with 171 Concertos by other composers, valued at four groschen apiece—a modest estimate!

These Concertos were Bach's first large-scale orchestral pieces, and were written in 1721, when he was thirty-six years of age.

These are not Concertos in the modern sense of the word, i.e. compositions for some solo instrument with Orchestra. The usual scheme of a Bach-period Concerto was that of a symphonic piece in which the band was divided into two portions, which alternated in performance and sometimes combined. Bach showed his interest in variety of orchestral colour by writing his six Concertos for six different combinations, and in some of them he departed altogether from the Concerto idea, as for instance, in the case of the one recorded, which is written for three groups of three stringed instruments—

3 Violins,
3 Violas,
3 'Cellos,

plus—

Double-bass and Harpsichord.

The part for the last-named instrument was indicated merely by the usual figures (indicating the chords the player was to use) under the String Bass part, and, as it was in this case obviously intended as nothing beyond a mere filling-up, and was probably merely thoughtlessly added in conformity with the custom of the day, which kept a Harpsichord or Organ playing as a background to all kinds of music, it is nowadays usually omitted, as in the preparation of this Record.

This third Brandenburg Concerto is always recognized as one of the most remarkable of Bach's compositions, and as the finest of the group.

It consists of only two movements (instead of the usual three), and these are joined by two long-sustained chords, which Goossens, however, omits.

First Movement.

Practically the whole movement is fashioned out of two tiny *motifs*, this one—

And this (which is but a blossoming forth of the other)—

Note that almost everywhere throughout the piece the instruments are treated as three distinct groups: I, Violins; II, Violas; III, 'Cellos and Double-basses.

At the opening, we see the main theme given to all the Violins in unison, and two-part accompanying harmonies to the Violas in unison and the Violoncellos likewise in unison (with, of course, the Double-bass doubling them an octave lower).

At this point, as will at once suggest itself, Bach is not making use of the division of each section of his ten-part String choir into three groups, but later he avails himself of it in passages where he divides up one or more of his sections into its three constituents, as for instance this passage (it begins in the ninth bar of the piece and can easily be traced on the Record):

(The Violas, on the one hand, and the 'Cellos and Basses, on the other, have in the extract, as set forth above, been compressed into single staves so as to reduce the score from ten staves to five, and make it easier to read.)

Note that here, at one point, the Violins are divided into three, contrapuntally treated (with some 'imitation' going on amongst them), and the Violas into three, harmonically treated (playing in chords the first little *motif* of the piece). The 'Cellos and Basses are left undivided, merely supplying a firm bass to the whole.

(At the opening of the extract, however, it will be noted that it is the 'Cellos that are divided, the other instruments playing in group-unison.)

This will be sufficient to make clear Bach's method in this particular piece, but it may be added that he is often very ingenious in his inversions. For instance, what he gives to his three Violins at one moment, he will give to his three Violas the next, what he gives to his Violas at that first moment being then given to the Violins. Thus, the very passage just quoted is repeated four or five bars later, with the chordal Viola part transferred to the Violins an octave higher, and the running contrapuntal Violin parts transferred to the Violas an octave lower, the bass continuing as before. It is impossible to point out all these devices in a written description; readers interested must spend a couple of shillings on the score, and disentangle it for themselves, thus gaining the power to enjoy the many beauties of contrapuntal contrivance that they formerly overlooked.

Rather more than half-way through the movement it comes to a momentary full-close in B minor. Here the Records turn, and on resuming you will note a brief fugal treatment of this theme, which appears in all the three Violin parts in turn—

It will be noted that this 'Subject' is combined with the initial theme of the movement.

Bach's great biographer and commentator, Spitta, thus remarks on this passage:

'One passage (from bar 78 onwards) is as fine as anything in the whole realm of German instrumental music; the chief subject is given out in the second violin part, the first violin then starts an entirely new subject which next appears on the second violin, drawing in more and more instruments, and is at last taken up by the third violin and the third viola, and given out weightily on their G string; this is the signal for a flood of sound to be set free from all sides, in the swirl of which all polyphony is drowned for several bars.'

Except for the statement about 'drawing in more and more instruments', which I do not understand, this is a good description of the passage.

Second Movement.

This is the 'Part 3' of the Records (the First Movement, as already mentioned, having been divided by 'a turn-over', into Parts 1 and 2). It is a very bright, short movement, almost entirely developed out of this theme taken up in turn by various instruments.

The Movement falls into two sections—a shorter one and a longer, each marked to be repeated (in these Records, however, Hoeberg repeats only the second, longer section, Goossens only the shorter). The second and longer section will be found, upon close listening, to include in its course the whole of the first and shorter section, note for note, transposed from G major into E minor.

The First Section ends about $\frac{3}{4}$ inch from the outer rim. A full-close occurs, and the fact that something is ending cannot be missed. This section is then repeated by Goossens, on whose Record the Second Section begins about $1\frac{1}{2}$ inches from outer rim, and the minor transposition of the First Section embedded in it begins four bars later, i.e. nearly $\frac{1}{4}$ inch farther on.

Parry thus describes the whole Concerto:

'The third concerto is much the most remarkable of the group, as it really departs from the old conception of concertos and depends upon the remarkably rich effects which can be obtained by having three groups of three instruments (that is three violins, three violas, and three 'cellos) with double-bass and *continuo* to add to the sonority. The grouping of three instruments is maintained almost invariably throughout with astonishing effect so that the chord-passages of one group are constantly pitted against the chord-passages of another group, except where for variety and sonorous enforcement of some characteristic idea the three like instruments are massed in unison. The artistic conception is superb and superbly carried out, especially in the first movement. There is no slow movement, but only two long-sustained chords between the first and the brilliant last movement. This latter is in $\frac{12}{8}$ time and most vivacious, but not so interesting as the first, as it has less variety and less genuine force in the subject matter.'

Schweitzer makes these remarks upon the Brandenburg Concertos in general:

'The Brandenburg Concertos are the purest products of Bach's polyphonic style. Neither on the organ nor on the clavier could he have worked out the architecture of a movement with such vitality; the orchestra alone permits him absolute freedom in the leading and grouping of the obbligato voices.'

Two Large Polydor Records. (Berlin Orchestra.) 66014–5, 5*s.* 9*d.* each.

On the reverse of the second Record is the Wedding Procession from Rimsky-Korsakof's fantastic Opera *The Golden Cockerel*—a piquant titbit, only fairly recorded.

Two Large H.M.V. Records. (Royal Albert Hall Orchestra.) D. 683–4, 6*s.* 6*d.* each.

On the reverse of the second Record is what is usually known to-day as the 'Air on the G String' of Bach. Actually this is the Second Movement from Bach's Third Suite, in D. In 1871 Wilhelmj rearranged the piece in key C, as a Violin Solo with accompaniment for either Strings or Piano, directing that the Air itself should be played on the G String, and in this form it has been everywhere performed. It is a pity that the opportunity this Record offered was not made use of to restore to us the original version.

Hoeberg (Polydor) takes the First Movement at a pace which to some people will be far too slow and heavy. Yet I think that as one plays the Record one feels that he justifies the pace by the tremendous, unrelenting weight and rhythmic force which is gained. Greater clarity, too, is obtained than on the H.M.V. Record—but this indeed applies also to the Second Movement, though Hoeberg takes that at a very sprightly pace, thereby making the more effective contrast between the Movements. Both Companies' Violas are a little weak—Polydor's the less so, but their Second and Third Violins are hardly strong enough.

Printed Music. The Brandenburg Concerto loosely described on the label as 'in G' is the No. 3, for Strings (not the No. 4 in the same key, for Strings and 2 Flutes). The miniature full score is published by Goodwin & Tabb, at 2*s*.

RECORD No. 13

Song . . . . . *Lift up your heads* . . . . . Bach

GERVASE ELWES.

(Pianoforte accompaniment by F. B. Kiddle.)

Bach. *Lift up your heads.*

(Free Translation, as sung.[1])

Lift up your heads on high,
And play the man, ye people.
For your salvation's nigh.

Where flows fair Eden's river
God ye shall serve for ever.

(Original.)

Hebt euer Haupt empor,
Und seid getrost, ihr Frommen,
Zu eurer Seelen Flor.

Ihr sollt in Eden grünen,
Gott ewiglich zu dienen.

This is a vigorous song, scored in the original for 2 Violins, Violas and Continuo (i.e. a 'Figured Bass', from which the 'Cellos and Basses would play their line of notes and the Harpsichordist work out extemporaneously an accompaniment—see page 32). It is one of those songs in which the instrumental part is as important as the voice part. It opens with a twelve-bar instrumental passage, and closes with the same passage, which means that there is nearly as much purely

[1] For the First Edition of this book I was unable to identify some of the words as sung by even this great singer. A reader has since kindly supplied the missing words from one of Elwes's programmes, and these have now been checked with the Record and added.

instrumental music as vocal music in the piece. Moreover, the swinging semiquaver rhythm of this tune persists all the time, either in the voice-part or the accompaniment.

There is a short middle modulatory section, in which the 'Relative Minor' key is for a time prominent (it begins where the words 'Where flows fair Eden's river' are first heard), but even through this the same rhythm and the same *motifs* are continuously used, so that the whole thing is bound together as one long, unbroken expression of the same musical thought.

Large Columbia Record. L. 1325, 6*s*. 6*d*. (On the reverse is Frank Bridge's *Love went a-riding*, recorded by the same singer.)

Printed Music. This song will be found in the Cantata 'Watch and Pray'; the separate song is published as No. 7 of Prout's edition of 'Songs and Airs by Bach' (Augener, 1*s*. 6*d*.).

Pianoforte Solo . *Prelude and Fugue in C* . . . . Bach
(No. 1 of the '48'.)
BUSONI.

Bach. *Prelude and Fugue in C.*

THE PRELUDE

This, the simplest of all the Preludes of Bach's '48', is also one of the most beautiful. It is throughout merely a succession of arpeggiated chords. Busoni's playing is perfect.

THE FUGUE

The Fugue is in four 'Voices'. It has no Countersubject. And it is the only Fugue of Bach's '48' entirely without an Episode.

Almost the whole Fugue is Stretto, i. e. one voice entering with the Subject before another has ceased. Here is an example:

At the end is an effective example of 'Pedal', i.e. a standing note in the bass, over which the other 'voices' maintain their motion:

A piece of this kind may be played in many different ways, and all good. Both in the Prelude and the Fugue Busoni has preferred a slow meditativeness to a rapid brilliance.

Large Columbia Record. L. 1445, *6s. 6d.* (on reverse Chopin's Étude in E minor, Op. 25, No. 5, by the same performer).

Printed Music. Editions of the '48' abound.

Concerto in D minor, for Two Violins . . . . Bach

(Columbia) ARTHUR CATTERALL AND JOHN S. BRIDGE,
with Orchestra conducted by Sir Hamilton Harty,
or
(Vocalion) ADILA FACHIRI AND JELLY D'ARANYI,
with Orchestra conducted by Stanley Chapple.

This is a very fine three-movement work, for two solo Violins and Strings.

In the score the word *Tutti* (= 'all', meaning, speaking generally, the whole Orchestra) will be found attached to many passages, others being marked *Solo*: in the *Tutti* portions the solo instruments play with the rest.

The Movements are as follows:

Vivace (= Lively),
Largo ma non tanto (= Slow, but not too much so),
Allegro (= Bright and quick).

First Movement.

The interest of this movement lies in happily bustling tunes, taken up in alternation by the two Violin parts (whether those parts happen for the moment to be *Tutti* parts or Solo parts).

Sometimes one Solo Violin gives out a theme, which is then taken up, almost in Fugal style by the other. At the opening the following theme is first given out by Second Violins (*Tutti*), and then by First Violins (*Tutti*), five notes higher (quite as in a Fugue exposition, except that there is an accompaniment for Violas and 'Cellos and Basses going on all the time):

(This theme is important; it often recurs and may be looked upon as the chief theme of the piece.)

Often there is some simple but effective bit of 'imitation', as here, where Second Violins have a little half-bar *motif*, which is then imitated by First Violins, and again taken up by Second Violins, this time in what is practically an 'inversion' (i.e. where notes went up before now they go down, and where they went down before now they go up).

Soon after this the chief theme is heard again in Second Violin, and then in First Violin (bars 14 and 18; the Second Violin entry in bar 14 needs listening for).

Then (bar 22—about one inch from outer edge) the Solo First Violin has this theme, taken up four bars later by Solo Second Violin:[1]

[1] If you are using the Miniature Full Score you will find an error, the engraver having begun to bring in the second violin a bar too soon, thought better of it, dropped it, and then brought it in again at the proper place.

A little later (bars 38 and 42) the same theme is given out by Second Solo Violin and then by First Solo Violin.

Then (bar 46) the *Tutti* Violins enter again for four bars with the first theme of the piece in the First Violins.

With the return to the Solo Violins, use is made of a new theme related to the wide-leaping one recently introduced, with an arpeggio figure against it in its companion part.

This comes first as shown above, and then with the parts reversed, and then, four bars from its introduction, another *Tutti* begins.

So the movement continues. It is unnecessary to analyse it to the end, as its style and material have been fully indicated. The lowbrow who can listen to this sort of music and think that Bach 'lacks melody', and the highbrow who can listen to it and take interest only in the mechanics of its construction are to be equally pitied—if they exist, which is very doubtful.

Second Movement.

This is a very famous Movement. Parry's description of it, in his *John Sebastian Bach, the Story of the Development of a Great Personality*, is worth quotation:

'In the well-known concerto in D minor for two violins and orchestra the slow movement is again, by a very long way, the most attractive feature of the work. It is quite possible that it stands absolutely in the front rank of all Bach's movements whose reason of existence is pure beautiful melody. But in this case the psychological element is not so much in evidence. Bach's mind was not in this case moved by the possibilities of such a contrast as that between the basses and the solo violin in the other concertos, but by the aesthetical possibilities of alternation between two solo violins, in which the cue would not be so much in apposition or contrast, but in sisterly discourse. Here is a case in which Bach, probably unconsciously, was carried by the force of circumstances in the direction of the modern conception of the concerto, for in making use of the qualities of the two solo violins ample material was supplied for the development of the whole movement, and consequently the orchestra comes to occupy a very subordinate and insignificant position, mainly contenting itself with supplying the harmonies and indicating the rhythmic pulse.'

As hinted in this extract, the Solo Violins play throughout, the other Violins everywhere forming a mere part of the accompanying body. This is, in fact, a Violin Duet with String Accompaniment.

No further description is needed.

Third Movement.

In spirit and style and construction this is so like the First Movement as to call for little description.

The Solo Violins (with accompaniment by the rest of the instruments) begin in imitation at a mere beat's distance:

and with this and other little themes they keep the game going for some time, e.g.:

and

A passage that comes twice in the Movement, and that is different in style from any previously heard in this Concerto, is one where the two Solo Violins repeat quaver four-note chords (each violin in double stopping) whilst the orchestral strings run about playfully in semiquavers.

It is, by the way, a slight defect in these Records that the timid conductors have been unable to bring themselves to provide more than a background for their two soloists, even in a place like the one just mentioned, where those soloists' functions are rather those of accompaniment and the part of the other Strings is melodically the more important. Such timidity is very common in Gramophone recording, vocal soloists especially being too kindly treated—as though *Vox et praeterea nihil* were the motto of the Recording Angel. But despite the fault of undue deference to the great in the present Records, they are undoubtedly part of the dozen one would pick if that were the meagre allowance with which one were to be placed upon a desert island.

Three large Columbia Records. L. 1613–5, each 6*s.* 6*d.*, *or* **Two large Vocalion Records.** A. 0252–3, each 5*s.* 6*d.* There is little to choose between the two recordings. Each is complete, though Columbia takes three Records to Vocalion's two. The Vocalion performance is more forceful and brilliant, but the Columbia has perhaps a little more subtlety, and its Orchestra is not *quite* so much in the background. Columbia might therefore prove preferable in the long run. On the last side of the Columbia Records is the pleasant Finale of Spohr's Duet in D major for Two Violins.

Printed Music. Augener's Edition, No. 7942, 4*s.*, and several other editions, give the accompaniment parts arranged for piano. The Miniature Full Score of the work, as it is played in this Record, is now published (Goodwin & Tabb, 2*s.*).

RECORD No. 18

Harpsichord Solos . { *Fugue in D minor* . . . . . Bach
{ *Fugue in E minor* . . . . . ,,

MRS. GORDON WOODHOUSE.

Bach. *Fugue in D Minor.*

This is a very interesting Fugue in three Voices, which we will call Soprano, Alto, and Bass.[1] The Subject (a long one) is given above.

In the Exposition of the Fugue the voices enter in the order, Alto, Soprano, Bass.

There is a Countersubject, and as it usually appears (above or below the Subject) in succeeding entries it may be worth noticing. It is here shown on its first appearance, with the Subject[2] above it:

[1] Once or twice (irregularly) it runs momentarily into four voices.

[2] Here, to be exact, called the 'Answer'.

When the Subject has made its first entry in all the three Voices (in other words, when the Exposition is ended) we have a succession of further (single) entries of the Subject, in various keys, separated by shorter or longer Episodes. Altogether there are eight such entries, and usually both Subject and Countersubject will be heard (or, shall we say? are there to be heard).

Then, at bar 67, which is about an inch from the inner circle, begins a long rush-about Cadenza, which may be authentic or may be an interpolation by some other hand than that of the composer, but, anyhow, is very exhilarating. A few bars of contrasted sobriety close the piece.

The Fugue has no Stretto, and no Pedal. On the whole it is not a very strict (or 'scientific') Fugue. But it is pleasurable, having attractions that soon grow on one.

If you want to study this Fugue carefully, and to learn to hear two or more 'Voices' at once, slow down the Gramophone, and take particular passages over and over again, until you feel you can hear everything. Then during several further hearings gradually speed the Gramophone up, until you have it at normal.

Bach. *Fugue in E Minor.*

The construction of this Fugue is so like that of the one just described that little need be said about it.

It is, like the other, a Three-Voice Fugue.

After the Subject has been announced in the Alto, we hear it immediately repeated (or 'answered') in the Soprano, with a Countersubject against it, thus :

Then we hear the Subject in the Bass, with the Countersubject in the Alto, and an added part in the Soprano.

Note that in the Exposition, whichever voice has 'sung' the Subject follows on with the Countersubject, whilst the Subject (or 'Answer') appears, above or below it, in some newly entering voice.

This Fugue also has no Stretto anywhere and no Pedal.

Until after repeated hearings the listener is likely to miss many entries of the Subject—especially those in the middle or lower voice. It is because one gradually and subconsciously learns to pick out such things that a Fugue (like any other involved piece of music) becomes more enjoyable as one knows it better. And this process of increasing appreciation can be speeded by some little conscious study, such as is implied in these notes.

Large H.M.V. Record. D. 491, *6s. 6d.*

Printed Music. Peters Edition, No. 210, contains the Fugue in E minor, and No. 212 the Fugue in D minor. (Each volume contains a number of other pieces of Bach, and costs 4*s.*)

RECORD No. 19

Vocal Solo . . { Recit. *Frondi tenere* / Air . *Ombra mai fu* } . . . Handel

(From *Serse* [1].)

CARUSO.

(Orchestral accompaniment.)

Recitative. Frondi tenere e belle del mio platano amato, per voi risplenda il fato. Tuoni, lampi e procelle, non v'oltraggino mai la cara pace, nè giunga a profanarvi austro rapace!

Ombra mai fu
Di vegetabile
Cara ed amabile
Soave più.

TRANSLATION

Recitative. Tender and beautiful leaves of my beloved plane-tree, for you may fate shine brightly. May thunder, lightning, and storms never outrage your dear peace, nor the fierce south wind profane you!

Air. Never was verdant shadow sweeter.

As was the operatic custom of the time, a piece of lyrical musical expression is preceded by a piece of declamation—

[1] Or 'Xerxes'.

an Air by a Recitative. The Air is, in various instrumental forms, one of the most familiar pieces in existence, under the title, 'Handel's Celebrated Largo'. It has never been surpassed for dignified expressiveness.

Caruso's singing of this piece is magnificent, given the Italian ideal, but from a sober British point of view passionate explosions, however much justified in the Recitative by allusions to thunder and lightning, would be better replaced in the Air by a spirit of repose. 'It is good to have a giant's voice, but not to use it like a giant.'

Large H.M.V. Record. D.B. 133, 8*s*. 6*d*. (On the reverse Sullivan's unfortunately so-imperfectly-*Lost Chord*.)

Printed Music. Novello, Italian words, 1*s*. 6*d*. Augener, Italian and English words (Recit. 'Tender foliage', and Arioso, 'No sylvan shade'), in D flat, E flat, or F, 1*s*. 6*d*. Joseph Williams, Italian and English words, 2*s*.

RECORDS Nos. 20 AND 21

Violin and Piano Duet *Fourth Sonata in D major* . . . Handel

ISOLDE MENGES.[1]

This is a four-movement Sonata of the older type (i.e. it knows nothing of the 'Sonata Form' of Haydn, Mozart, and Beethoven).

There are four contrasted movements as follows: slow, quick, slow, quick, on the labels of the Record described as:

Andante sostenuto (= Pretty slow, and sustained),
Allegro (= Bright and quick),
Larghetto (= Rather slow),
Allegro con brio (= Quick and with spirit).

First Movement.

The feature of this is a long-drawn, lavishly ornamented, and very expressive violin melody, based a good deal upon the rhythm of the *motif* marked (2) in the extract given above.

[1] The pianist is not mentioned upon the label of the Record. Why?

The Movement is in 'Simple Binary' Form. It begins in key D major, and in the middle comes to a momentary rest in the dominant key, i.e. A major.

At this point the Record omits two bars of keyboard interlude.

Then it begins again, with the same material as at the opening, but this time in the new key, A, modulates through various related keys and works its way back to the 'home key' D.

As it approaches the end a good deal is made of the initial *motif* (marked (1) above). Just as it is settling, apparently finally, into the home key, an unexpected bar is added, leading into key A again, so producing an inconclusive effect and an expectancy for the

Second Movement.

The best way of giving a general description of this Movement is to say that it consists of a number of lively themes, each introduced by one instrument and then taken up by the other.

For instance, listen carefully as the opening passage (given above) is played, and you will notice that it has this bass:

Immediately afterwards (beginning at bar 5) you will find this reversed, what was the Keyboard Bass now becoming the Violin part, and what was the Violin part becoming the Keyboard Bass.

Find out for yourself what happens in the next little stretch of music (i.e. bars 9–12), and then note the entry of a passage in the Violin based upon this *motif*:

with this bass:

This goes on for four bars, and then (at bar 17) the parts are reversed as before.

Other *motifs* are taken up from time to time, not always in this change-and-change-about way but in simple 'imitation', but the themes quoted are the most important, and the hints that have been given as to the way Handel has treated his material are sufficient to help the listener to make use of a very good opportunity for sharpening his ears. Any one who has gone through this Movement carefully sufficiently often to feel sure he has heard all there is in it has given himself a very useful piece of listening practice.

Third Movement.

This is simply a slow, long-drawn Violin melody with Keyboard accompaniment. It is, for relief, in a Minor Key (the Relative Minor=B).

Note Handel's familiar device of an added four bars at the end, closing on a chord of expectancy. It almost looks as though he interposed these inconclusive phrases (compare end of First Movement) to balk the people in any audience who like to break a Sonata or String Quartet or Symphony into four fragments by clapping every movement, or perhaps, to balk the performers who like to get up and bow after every Movement.

Fourth Movement.

This is just a lively dance-like tune, very sequential in character. (Bars 3 and 4 above show what is meant by a 'Sequence'—a repetition of a *motif* or a phrase at a higher or lower pitch.)

The Movement is in the so common (at that period) Simple Binary Form. Its First Part begins in Key D and ends in Key A (i.e. the Dominant Key): its Second Part then begins in A, modulates a good deal, and then works back to D.

Each part is marked by the composer to be played twice, and is so played in this Record.

The whole Movement is thoroughly happy.

Note the admirable contrast amongst the four Movements of this Sonata.

Two small H.M.V. Records. E. 279-80, each 4*s*. 6*d*.

Printed Music. A convenient edition is that of Wessely (Joseph Williams, Berners Edition, No. 538, 2*s*.), though the piano part of this differs in some details from that used in making the Record. (As at this period composers indicated their keyboard parts by a mere figured-bass, modern editions, in which it has been worked out in full, necessarily vary.)

RECORD No. 22

Vocal Solos . . *Where'er you walk* . . . . Handel
(From the Opera *Semele.*)
Deeper, and deeper still.
(From the Oratorio *Jephtha.*)
FRANK MULLINGS.
(With Orchestral accompaniment.)

Handel. *Where'er you walk.*

Where'er you walk cool gales shall fan the glade,
Trees, where you sit, shall crowd into a shade;
Where'er you tread the blushing flow'rs shall rise,
And all things flourish where'er you turn your eyes.

This is simply a lovely air, in Ternary Form (i.e. a first strain, a second strain, and the first repeated). It is typical Handel of the serener type.

Handel. *Deeper, and deeper still.*

Recitative.

Deeper, and deeper still, thy goodness, child,
Pierceth a father's bleeding heart, and checks
The cruel sentence on my faltering tongue.
Oh! let me whisper it to the raging winds,
Or howling deserts; for the ears of men
It is too shocking.—Yet—have I not vow'd?
And can I think the great Jehovah sleeps,
Like Chemosh, and such fabled deities?
Ah! no: heav'n heard my thoughts and wrote them down—
It must be so.—'Tis this that racks my brain,
And pours into my breast a thousand pangs,
That lash me into madness.—Horrid thought!—
My only daughter!—so dear a child,
Doom'd by a father!—Yes—the vow is past,
And Gilead hath triumph'd o'er his foes.—
Therefore, to-morrow's dawn—I can no more!

This is a very finely impressive piece of intense tragic feeling, and Mr. Mullings sings it with immense fire, though one wishes he would not seek a melodramatic effect with such explosive endings as 'sentence-e', 'Chemosh-e', and 'deities-e', and that the orchestra accompanying him were less feebly distant in effect.

Detailed knowledge of the Old Testament being less common now than it used to be, and becoming still less common every year, the 'Argument' of the Oratorio, taken from the standard Novello edition, is here appended—up to the point where this Recitative occurs.

The Israelites, who for their idolatry had been oppressed by the Ammonites for eighteen years, become repentant and invite Jephtha, a son of Gilead, to be their Captain in the war with their enemies. He accepts the trust, and (after a valedictory interview with his wife), in the ardour of his desire for victory, offers up to God a vow, that if he should return home a conqueror, whatsoever cometh forth out of his house to meet him, shall be dedicated to the Lord; which is followed by a general invocation of the mercy and blessing of the Almighty. His wife in his absence being troubled with forebodings of some pending evil, her daughter attempts to dispel her gloomy apprehensions. In the following scene, Jephtha, having failed in his attempts to secure peace by a treaty, arouses the army of Israel for the battle.

News being brought to Iphis of her father's victory, she resolves to go out to meet him on his return. Zebul celebrates the happiness resulting from the triumph that had been gained, and is joined by Jephtha, who commends the valour of his chiefs, but piously ascribes the glory of the event to God,—whose Omniscience and Omnipotence are celebrated by a chorus of the people. Jephtha is then met by his daughter and a train of virgins, who welcome his return with music and dancing. Struck with horror and despair at the sight, he makes known his vow;—his friends expostulate with him;—his daughter resigns her fate to his will;—he is torn with anguish and remorse, but resolves on the fulfilment of his vow.

To maintain the feeling of terror in a long slow Recitative like this is a triumph for composer and performer. A good deal of the former's success is due to the bold harmonic and modulatory scheme. To define precisely through what keys this piece passes in the course of its forty bars would be difficult, as it sometimes hovers on the edge of a new key and then retreats in some other direction (it may be described as a masterpiece of inconclusive modulation), but the key-scheme is something like this (small letters for minor keys, large for major):—f sharp, b, e, d, a, F, g, c, f, b flat, A flat, G, f, G. Any one who knows a little about the older harmony and its key relationships will realize the harmonic and modulatory courage here shown.

Large Columbia Record. L. 1344, 6*s.* 6*d.*

Printed Music. *Where'er you walk* is published by Novello in B♭ at 8*d.*, and in A♭ (School Songs 740) at 2*d.* The Oratorio *Jephtha* is published at 4*s.*; *Deeper, and Deeper still* is published separately at 1*s.*, or can be had in Randegger's *Twelve Handel Songs for Tenor* (3*s.*). Publisher in all these forms, Novello.

RECORD No. 23

Vocal Solos . { *O Sleep, why dost thou leave me?* (From the Oratorio *Semele.*) *Angels ever bright and fair* (From the Oratorio *Theodora.*) } . . Handel

ALMA GLUCK.

(With Orchestral accompaniment.)

Handel. *O Sleep, why dost thou leave me?*

O Sleep, why dost thou leave me?
Why thy visionary joys remove?
O Sleep, again deceive me,
To my arms restore my wandering love.

This is simply a beautiful air, beautifully performed, and there is nothing to say about it.

Handel. *Angels ever bright and fair.*

Angels ever bright and fair,
Take, O take me to your care.
Speed to your own courts my flight,
Clad in robes of virgin white.

Handel used to maintain that his Oratorio *Theodora* contained some of his finest work. But its career began badly, when in March, 1750, London was suffering from an earthquake scare; and it is now known to most people only by *Angels ever bright and fair*—one of Handel's simplest, most attractive Soprano Airs.

Large H.M.V. Record. D.B. 278, 8*s*. 6*d*.

Printed Music. Editions of *O Sleep* (with English words) are to be had of Novello and Augener, each 1*s*.

Editions of *Angels ever bright and fair* abound.

RECORDS Nos. 24 AND 25

String Quartet in B flat, Op. 64, *No.* 3 . . . . . . Haydn

THE LONDON STRING QUARTET.

This Quartet has four Movements as follows:

Vivace assai,
Adagio,
Menuetto,
Finale—Allegro con spirito.

First Movement.

This is a very bright and lively Movement. It begins:

This soon follows:

This material makes up the First Subject of the Movement. The Second Subject begins thus:

There follows a passage in which the First Violin gives out the opening *motif* of the piece alternately with the Second Violin and Viola (in 10ths), and the first section of the piece works on, largely by means of scales, to its close, which takes place *pianissimo*. This section is marked to be repeated, but the command is usually unobserved, and so it is in this Record.

The Development of this material follows, and very effective it is, partly because the material is so varied and contrasted.

Then, after a passage of a sort of mock-resumption of the First Subject, in the Minor, the piece actually returns in the Major. Here then, at last (about half an inch from the inner circle), is the Recapitulation. But it is unusually brief, does not contain the Second Subject, and is made still briefer by the omission of about twenty bars near the end, in order to get it into the Record.

Second Movement.

This is an Air with Variations.

The Air opens:

It has a second part beginning:

(In the score each of these parts is immediately repeated in an embellished form; in the Record the repetitions are omitted. If you have the score before you cross out bars 8–16 and 24–32, and so save yourself from disappointment.)

Variation 1 is in the Minor. The First Violin part is very active in decorative passages, through which the original Air can be discerned (bars 41–50, which repeat this with slight further embellishments, are 'cut').

Then the second part of the Air is varied, also in the Minor.

Variation 2. Back in the Major. A simple and graceful slight ornamentation of the original Air, in its two parts. Triplets are a new rhythmic feature that soon enters into this Variation.

(Bars 70–82 are 'cut'.)

There follows a CODA—short and effective.

The several references above to passages 'cut' may give the impression that the performance is spoilt. This is by no means the case; it will be readily understood that an Air with Variations stands excision better than most forms, and even as thus reduced the Movement remains a thing of great beauty. Its special feature is perhaps the rich and often very chromatic harmony.

Third Movement.

This is a very dainty Movement. It consists of Minuet-Trio-Minuet, in other words of two Minuets arranged first-second-first. Each of the two Minuets consists of two parts.

Of the first Minuet the first part begins as shown above. This part is only fourteen bars long, and is repeated. The second part is much longer, and begins very strikingly on Viola and 'Cello, imitating what the First Violin (with double-stopping) has just done in closing the previous part,

and includes at the end a repetition of the first part, with a short Coda.

(The repeat marked for the whole of this is not, in this performance, observed.)

The Second Minuet (= 'Trio', but how absurd we are to speak of 'the Trio of a Quartet'!) begins as follows:

Its plan is precisely that of the First Minuet.

Haydn is here very light in touch and this is a delightful piece of work. Syncopation is a feature almost throughout.

After the Second Minuet the First one is repeated.

Fourth Movement.

This begins with a flippantly gay little tune as its First Subject:

This subject grows to some length, and is continued by a 'Bridge', which has several striking features, in especial some bars of light staccato quaver chords followed by *pianissimo* minim chords, and then, after a loud *sforzando*, by a merry passage which leads us into the Second Subject:

So we come to the end of the Exposition.

The Development follows, and is worth careful listening in order to observe its treatment of the material already given out.

The opening of the Recapitulation (about an inch from inner circle) is easy to find. It repeats the Exposition almost exactly (except for the necessary change of key of the Second Subject).

The whole concludes with a short Coda fashioned out of the First Subject.

Two large Vocalion Records. D. 02020 and D. 02039, each 4*s*. 6*d*.

Printed Music. Miniature Score, Goodwin & Tabb, 1*s*. 6*d*., here called on the title-page, Op. 64, No. 3, though, as a matter of fact, Haydn did not attach 'opus' numbers to his compositions.

RECORD No. 26

Vocal Solo . . . *With verdure clad* . . . . Haydn

(From the Oratorio, *The Creation.*)

BESSIE JONES *or* FLORENCE AUSTRAL.

(Each with Orchestral accompaniment.)

With verdure clad the fields appear,
Delightful to the ravish'd sense;
By flowers sweet and gay
Enhanced is the charming sight,
Here fragrant herbs their odours shed;
Here shoots the healing plant.[1]

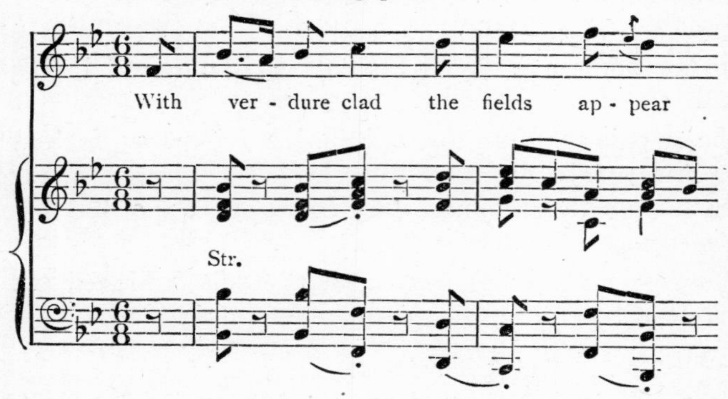

This is an air sung by the Angel Gabriel in Haydn's *Creation.*[2] The persons of the Oratorio are Gabriel, Archangel, Uriel, Raphael, Adam and Eve, and a Chorus of Angels.

The following, from the preface to Sir George Macfarren's edition of the Oratorio, describes the present extract:

'Gabriel, who was the guardian of Paradise in Rabbinical tradition, tells of the adornment of the earth with vegetation; the beautiful Air

---

[1] These are the words sung on both Records. I find it impossible to discover the words of what, later in this description, I call the 'Development Section', as sung by Bessie Jones.

[2] For a note concerning this Oratorio see p. 129.

which is an outpouring of the composer's feelings on the contemplation of the sunlit landscape in its many-hued beauty, with the predominance of that warm colour on which the sight loves to repose, fulfils the plan of the first movement of an instrumental Sonata, having its first and second subjects, its elaboration of these, and its retrospect of its own earlier portion, and, according to Bombet, it is the third essay of the composer to do justice to the situation, and in this finished form was a special favourite with him.'

The passages Macfarren, quite plausibly, looks upon as two sonata 'Subjects' (for a full description of this type of design see p. 133) are that with which the piece opens and that which brings the words 'Here fragrant herbs'. Parts of the structure of this Vocal Sonata Movement are omitted in each of these Records.

In the Zonophone Record, bars 64–82 (inclusive) are cut; that is, the 'Second Subject' is not given its second hearing in the 'Recapitulation' (or 'retrospect', as Macfarren calls it). This is a very skilful and not very harmful cut. Austral's Record is definitely incomplete, omitting the whole of the 'Development' (Macfarren's 'elaboration' of the previous matter) and part of the Second Subject in the Recapitulation.

Bessie Jones's phrasing and general performance are not perfect, but seem the better. She holds one top note unwarrantably, and in her diction she gives us that weird version of the English language which so many Sopranos seem to affect. Many vowels are given a rather childlike brightness, presumably with the object of displaying brilliance of tone. 'Ravished' becomes 'rah-vish'd'; and if you wish to pronounce the German 'Schütz', copy Bessie Jones's English 'shoots'.

The light orchestration is a pleasure to listen to, and particularly the delicate treatment of the Clarinet. This is an instrument that came into common use in Haydn's lifetime. In many of his symphonies it is not included in the score; here he uses one Clarinet but no Oboe. It can be heard entering, three times, with a charming little curly interjection, during the first enunciation of the lines, 'By flowers sweet and gay enhanced is the charming sight'. On the later appearance of these lines, towards the end of the song, a delightful little touch of Flutes is an addition to the Clarinet curl.

The Zonophone Record belongs to the 'new recording', and has all its wonderful balance and clarity, but also its reedy Strings.

Large Zonophone Record (Bessie Jones). A. 299, 4*s*. (On the reverse, *I know that my Redeemer liveth*, considerably cut, from Handel's *Messiah*.)

Large H.M.V. Record (Florence Austral). D. 775, 6*s*. 6*d*. (On the reverse, *Softly sighs* from Weber's *Der Freischütz*.)

Printed Music. *The Creation* is published by Novello at 1*s*. 6*d*. (small size) and 3*s*. (large size); the separate song may be had of the same publishers at 1*s*.

RECORDS Nos. 27, 28, AND 29

The Surprise Symphony . . . . Haydn

Columbia—THE NEW QUEEN'S HALL ORCHESTRA, CONDUCTED BY SIR HENRY WOOD.
Polydor—THE ORCHESTRA OF CHARLOTTENBURG OPERA HOUSE, BERLIN, CONDUCTED BY LEO BLECH.
Parlophone—THE ORCHESTRA OF THE STATE OPERA HOUSE, BERLIN, CONDUCTED BY DR. WEISSMANN.

This is one of the Twelve Symphonies in which Englishmen may share some of the pride of ownership, since Haydn wrote them for a London Season, 1792.

The 'Surprise' Symphony owes its nickname to a moment in the Second Movement (it has four altogether) when the audience, having settled down somnolently to soft, slow music, is abruptly roused by a crash from the Full Orchestra, including a Kettledrum bang. (The work is known on the Continent as 'The Drumstroke Symphony'.)

Haydn here uses Flutes, Oboes, Bassoons, Horns, Trumpets, Kettledrums (two of each), and Strings.

First Movement.

The work opens with a brief grave Introduction (*Adagio cantabile*), in which smooth, expressive Woodwind and Strings are contrasted. Presently there come two sharp, loud chords, then a sustained one, then a tender gesture in First Violins.

Now the First Movement proper (*Vivace assai*) opens. It is in 'First Movement' Form (see p. 133). Here is the beginning of the First Subject:

That tiny, graceful violin tune is the core of the Movement. The loud fanfare in Full Orchestra which here follows it is somewhat prolonged. Violins boldly range high and low, while Wind instruments chiefly play chords, helping the Drums and the bass instruments to mark time. Suddenly the noise subsides, and Violins repeat their graceful tune, this time with a gentle comment from Oboe.

The Full Orchestra breaks forth again, Violins and Oboe repeat their strains, this time modified, and there comes yet another 'Tutti'.

Now at last comes the Second Subject. This begins something like a quick waltz:

There follows another short tune in Strings—the smoothest tune in the piece. Then we hear a delicious little phrase, beginning thus, in Flute and Oboes:

A short Tutti brings the Enunciation to an end.

In the early days of 'First Movement' or 'Sonata' Form it was usual to repeat the Enunciation. This was little more than a convention, to help listeners to grasp the material of the Movement. On the Columbia Record this repeat is not made. On the Parlophone and Polydor Records the First Side ends with the close of this Section.

The Development Section is only about half as long as the Enunciation. It begins with a little treatment of the First Subject, and is then chiefly occupied in bold, emphatic declamation.

By and by, the First Subject creeps back (on Columbia just after the beginning of Side 2), this time with First Flute an octave above First Violins, and with the Oboe's ejaculations.

The Recapitulation, which has now begun, is almost a repetition of the Enunciation. But notice how, in its course, the First Subject appears in two new, contrasting lights. At one time it is played strongly by Strings, later it forms a delicate Woodwind quartet, First Flute having the tune, Oboes and First Bassoon accompanying.

Second Movement.

This is an *Andante* (i.e. a fairly slow Movement), in the form of an Air with Variations. The Air begins:

Here, at the end of this quotation, is the sudden outbreak which gives the name to the whole Symphony.

The Air continues, after this, for another sixteen bars, and then we come to the **First Variation.** Here the First Violins play pleasant semiquavers above the Air, joined in one place by the Flute.

Second Variation. This is in the minor. It begins loudly, the Flutes, Oboes, and Bassoons, at the opening, joining the Strings, all in simple octaves.

Demisemiquaver scales, passing from one stringed instrument to another, soon become a feature, with long-held chords on Flute and Oboes. By and by the whole band is engaged. (All three Companies' Records turn over here.)

Third Variation. This returns to the major, the Air being at the outset given to the Oboe, which plays it in repeated semiquavers. Then the Air is given to the Violins, and Flute and Oboe play counterpoints above it.

Fourth Variation. Mostly loud. Full Orchestra. The Wind have the Air, and the Violins an embroidery.

A short CODA, founded on the initial *motif* of the Air, rounds off the Movement.

The whole thing is very charming in its naivety.

(Columbia omits three little repeats, in Variations 1 and 2.)

Third Movement.

This is a very sprightly, energetic Minuet and Trio.

The usual Minuet-Trio-Minuet plan is followed (cf. pp. 79–80, 95–6).

The Minuet opens thus:

To describe it would need a mass of quotations. It is wonderfully detailed, clever, agile, yet all runs along perfectly simply and spontaneously.

You feel that even the TRIO has flowed straight out of the Minuet. (If you study it, you may find that it has. For instance, its opening is an inversion of the opening of the second part of the Minuet.)

Here is its beginning; notice the delightful 'colour' produced by the playing of the tune by Violins and Bassoon at the octave:

Columbia starts Side 4 with the Trio.

Fourth Movement.

This opens with the First Subject as follows:

Soon the Flute takes up the same tune.

The Second Subject begins like this:

First Violins, repeated with Oboe added.

First Violins continue 8ve below Flute.

The Movement, we soon find, is in 'First Movement Form', and the Development opens with what sounds like a return to the First Subject, but it soon changes to a treatment of *motifs* derived from it.

Later it sounds as though the Recapitulation is beginning (where the same First Subject comes in three octaves, Flute, First Violin, and Bassoon, with accompaniment on the other Strings). Modulation to distant keys follows, however.

At last the actual Recapitulation opens—with the same instruments, by the way, as in the false one just mentioned. (Columbia takes in the first bit of the Recapitulation on Side 4, then for the beginning of Side 5 goes back again to the false start, thereby giving us two more false starts free of charge.) The First Subject is, after a time, followed by the Second, and a Coda ends all.

The device of raising expectancy and then disappointing it is very cleverly (and almost humorously) used by Haydn in this Movement.

The geniality of the whole thing is marked. It is all very typical of 'Papa Haydn'.

Three Large Columbia Records. L. 1668–70, 6*s.* 6*d.* each. (On the sixth side Järnefeldt's popular *Praeludium* is excellently recorded.)

or

Three Large Parlophone Records. E. 10242–4, 4*s.* 6*d.* each.

or

Three Large Polydor Records. 69723–5, 5*s.* 9*d.* each.

On their labels, Polydor ignore the fact that the First Movement proper is *Vivace assai* (not *Adagio cantabile*, which applies only to the Introduction) and incorrectly designate the Last Movement *Adagio di Molto*, instead of *Allegro di Molto*.

Parlophone is, on the whole, the most correct, and is excellently balanced and clear in the 'Tutti'. But Columbia has far more life and spirit, and has recorded splendidly all the spiciest bits—indeed, does almost full justice to Haydn's most delightful orchestral colouring. Polydor comes somewhere between the two, and might by some be considered a happy medium. Its worst failing is the slow pace and heaviness of the First Movement.

But if you forbear much criticism for the sake of real life and freshness, and wish to enjoy the best moments in the work most fully, get Columbia.

Printed Music. Miniature Full Score, Goodwin & Tabb, 2*s*.

RECORDS Nos. 30, 31, AND 32

String Quartet in D . . . . Haydn

(Called the 'Hornpipe Quartet'.)

THE SPENCER DYKE STRING QUARTET.

THE FLONZALEY QUARTET.

This piece has four Movements:

1. Allegro moderato (= Moderately quick).
2. Adagio cantabile (= Slow and in a singing style).
3. Menuetto; Allegretto (= Pretty quick).
4. Finale; Vivace (= Lively).

First Movement.

This opens in a particularly delightful way. Second Violin, Viola, and 'Cello begin to prowl around mincingly, in this fashion:

Soon (while they continue) the First Subject is heard, high up, in First Violin:

A little later this happy little *motif* creeps in (note it well, as it is much used from time to time throughout the movement):

By and by appears the Second Subject, a syncopated harmonic one:

The Exposition closes with a short Coda, partly consisting of a triplet descending-scale passage, which please note, partly of the happy little *motif* from the end of the First Subject.

The Exposition is marked to be repeated, but this direction is (in music of this kind and period) little more than a formality which is often, as here, disregarded nowadays.

Now opens the Development, which at first treats the First Subject, then the triplet-scale passage just mentioned (which now sometimes runs down hill and sometimes up), and then the Second Subject, then (just after three mysterious chords) another triplet passage derived from the one previously heard and played (in three octaves) by all the instruments together.

Suddenly this subsides, as back come those stealthy footsteps which first led forth the First Subject. This is played as it was first given out, then Haydn dashes off again into the triplet runs. He also gives us slower, gliding phrases, which, like the run-about passages, come from the Coda of the Exposition—possibly they are hinted at still earlier. Presently there comes a pause; then the First Subject is heard once again. This time it is immediately followed by the Second Subject, and the Recapitulation ends with the little Coda which closed the Exposition.

Second Movement.

This is a brief but very lovely song-like movement.

The first portion (34 bars) contains a tune in the major key, played by the First Violin. Note the beautiful sweeps up the scale to its two highest notes, A and C♯, in bars 4 and 12 respectively.

Then (at bar 17) comes a minor section with a beautiful momentary melting into the major at its fourth bar; then the return of the original tune, a couple of bars later. This is cut short, and, with half a dozen bars to round it off, ends the first part of the movement.

The middle part is very short indeed—only 16 bars. It is really only a link to join on the varied and ornamented form of the first tune, which concludes the movement. Here the Flonzaley Quartet cut out 22 bars (i.e. the opening major tune and the minor section), and go straight to the concluding return of the original tune (now, as I have said, ornamented).

Third Movement (Minuet and Trio).

The construction is: Minuet—Trio—Minuet again. Each portion has two strains, which are marked to be repeated. (The usual plan as to repetitions in a Minuet and Trio is as follows: (*a*) Minuet in two sections, each repeated as it occurs; (*b*) Trio in two sections, each repeated as it occurs; (*c*) Minuet again, this time without any repetition of the sections.)

The movement begins with a wide-ranging tune, the first notes of the first two bars having each a piquant crushed note (= *Acciaccatura*) which has almost the effect of a wink, and gives the passage a touch of gay impudence. In the second strain, towards the end, these crushed notes are tossed up and down, three in a bar.

The Trio grows spontaneously out of the upward scale of the Minuet, thus:

But it is in the minor mode, and is altogether quite a contrast to the Minuet. It has more scale work, the Second Violin giving out a running phrase, which is taken up by First Violin, four bars later; three bars after that the 'Cello begins the rhythm, and one bar later the Viola is at it. The second strain keeps up the same rhythmical run of six quavers in a bar.

Then the Minuet comes back, exactly as at first.

Fourth Movement (Finale).

This is the Hornpipe from which the Quartet is named. It is very straightforward, and its rhythm runs along in eight semiquavers to the bar almost all the way through.

The first section has the tune in the First Violin part, the other instruments accompanying with short detached chords, or joining in a duet for a few bars (as does the Second Violin near the end of this section).

Then, in the Minor Key, comes a middle portion, starting off in duet form (First and Second Violins), the Second accompanying the First with a rhythmic figure similar to that of the opening bars of the Hornpipe.

Then, after four bars, the parts are reversed, and the Second Violin has the tune. The 'Cello joins in at the tenth bar of this section, and the Viola four bars later, so that the whole is in the style of the opening of a Fugue, the instruments chasing each other with the same tune.

After all have had a turn at it, the First Violin has an extra turn, and then the idea is developed a little, Violins I and II chasing each other with a little two-note leaping figure, a fragment of the subject. The former then rollicks down two octaves with a little pattern, and climbs up again, finally being left by itself to creep quietly back into the Hornpipe again, the others striking in with the *staccato* accompaniment, as at the start.

There is a longish tail-piece, or Coda. The short all-in-a-breath race of the First Violin in the last bars, with the Second Violin and Viola running down hill, and all trying to get to their destinations first, is very jolly. This Movement is recorded complete (including both 'repeats').

Three small Vocalion Records. X. 9554-6, each 3*s*.

The first two Movements are played by the Flonzaley Quartet on a **Large H.M.V. Record,** DB. 250, 8*s*. 6*d*.

This is a fine example of the beautiful *ensemble* of the Flonzaley Quartet (it is said that their four instruments were all made, centuries ago, by the same maker—it is well to order such things well in advance, so that they may have time to mature!). Also they take the First Movement much quicker than do the Spencer Dyke Quartet, and give a delightful performance in the real Haydn spirit. Their Second Movement, too, has greater feeling; their 'cut' (described on page 95), though not a mortal wound, is somewhat disfiguring. The Spencer Dyke Quartet play the first two Movements flawlessly, but, I think, tamely. I recommend the H.M.V. Record of the first two Movements, and the Vocalion Record of the last two.

Printed Music. Miniature Score, Goodwin & Tabb, described as 'Op. 64, No. 5' (see remark, p. 81), 1*s*.

RECORD No. 33

Vocal Duet . . . *Là ci darem la mano* . . . . Mozart

(From the Opera *Don Giovanni*.)

Rosa Raisa and Giacomo Rimini.

(Orchestral accompaniment.)

Mozart. *Là ci darem.*

Don Juan. Là ci darem la mano,
Là mi dirai di sì;
Vedi non è lontano,
Partiam, ben mio, da qui!

Zerlina. Vorrei, e non correi,
Mi trema un poco il cor:
Felice è ver sarei,
Ma può burlarmi ancor!

Don Juan. Vieni, mio bel diletto!
Zerlina. Mi fa pietà Masetto!
Don Juan. Io cangierò tua sorte!
Zerlina. Presto, non son più forte.
Don Juan. Vieni!

Both. Andiam, mio bene,
A ristorar le pene
D'un innocente amor!

Mozart's *Don Giovanni*, properly a comic opera, and perfectly hideous if seriously played, tells, of course, the story of the traditional betrayer, who ranged the world in his busy activities, and came to a bad and brimstony end.

Là ci darem la mano is a duet between Don Giovanni and a country girl. In order to have an opportunity of making love to her he has arranged a party at his villa for a group of peasants including her and her betrothed (Masetto).

Here is a free translation of the words, as taken from E. J. Dent's excellent acting version, many times performed in London, at the 'Old Vic.' theatre:

Giov. You'll lay your hand in mine, dear,
Softly you'll whisper, 'Yes',
'Tis not so far to go, dear,
Your heart is mine, confess.
Zerlina. What answer shall I make him?
My heart will not be still.
I'd love to be a lady—
Surely he means no ill.
Giov. Come then, my fairest treasure!
Zer. Masetto 'll ne'er forgive me.
Giov. I'll give you wealth and pleasure.
Zer. Surely you'll not deceive me?
Both. Where youth and love invite us,
With pleasure to delight us,
Of joy we'll make our fill.
Giov. You'll come?
Zer. I will.

(ELVIRA *bursts in upon them and warns* ZERLINA.)

Small Vocalion Record (Raisa and Rimini). B. 3100, 4*s.*

On the reverse Rimini sings the fine Drinking Song, *Inaffia l'ugola-trinca tra canna*, from Verdi's *Otello*, without, of course, the chorus, and with some cuts.

This Record has an orchestral accompaniment, which seems to depart very slightly and not seriously from the original score. The whole is very effective and pleasing. (Rimini gives us a good example of long phrasing.) Raisa and Rimini take a few liberties with the text—maybe they are 'traditional' modifications!

Printed Music. The vocal score of *Don Giovanni* is published by Novello at 5*s.* 6*d.* (paper), 7*s.* 6*d.* (cloth). The separate song can be obtained of the same publishers at 2*s.* 6*d.* (Italian words).

RECORDS Nos. 34, 35, AND 36

String Quartet in B flat (No. 15 or 4) . . . . . Mozart

LÉNER STRING QUARTET.

This is the Quartet which (Haydn and Mozart taking part) was played in the presence of Mozart's father Leopold, the last time father and son ever met; and that led old Haydn to solemnly avow to the old father that his son was the greatest composer known to him.

First Movement.

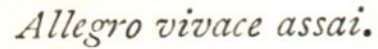

The Movement opens with a very artlessly happy First Subject which might almost, from its character and style, be one of Bach's comic songs in his *Peasant Cantata.* Everything is pellucid and little description is needed, but note that after about twenty-five bars the First Violin takes to trilling, whilst the under parts give out the tune just quoted. A good deal is then made of a 'catchy' little *motif*:

The following may probably be considered the Second Subject:

The Enunciation is repeated in full, and the First Side of the Record then ends.

The Development Section opens with a new tune:

The 'catchy' *motif* is then a good deal 'developed'—or rather a *motif* akin to it is.

Soon comes the Recapitulation, which is practically a note-for-note repetition of the Enunciation; just a few notes are changed, to bring the Second Subject and all the last part into the main key of the Movement.

Then there is a Coda which gives us a little final treatment of the First Subject and the 'catchy' *motif*.

Second Movement.

This is a rather sedate Minuet:

followed by an only slightly less sedate Trio:

After this the Minuet is, of course, repeated.

Third Movement.

This opens expressively:

The music continues on these lines, with embellishments added, in quicker notes, until there enters another Subject, a First Violin melody, beginning like this:

over repeated chords, played by the three lower instruments. A moment later the 'Cello takes this melody, the chords being given to the three instruments above it.

With Side 4 the First Subject returns and then in its turn the Second Subject, both of them much as first given out.

Fourth Movement.

This is a very pleasant little movement. It begins with the following frank tune:

and continues in this style for some time.

Several little tunes follow. Here is one of the most important:

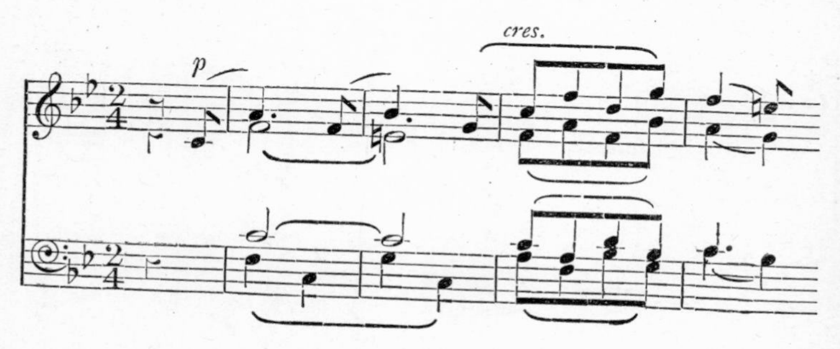

At last we come to a Cadence, and the Development Section opens. It is made out of previously heard material, which will be easily recognized.

Then the First Subject returns, and we have entered upon the Recapitulation, in which there is practically nothing new.

Three large Columbia Records. L. 1606–8, each 6*s.* 6*d.*

Printed Music. The miniature score is published by Goodwin & Tabb at 1*s.* 6*d.* (it is the one described on its title-page as No. 4, though described on the Record as No. 15). The various unofficial numberings of works of Haydn and Mozart are a nuisance; these composers did not use 'Opus numbers', and it is much to be wished that everybody would accept the standard (Köchel Catalogue) numeration for all Mozart works. In this the one just described is No. 458.

RECORD No. 37

Vocal Solo . . *Deh, vieni, non tardar* . . . Mozart
(From the Opera *Le Nozze di Figaro.*)

(Vocalion) KATHLEEN DESTOURNEL (with the Aeolian Orchestra).
(H.M.V.) GRAZIELLA PARETO (with Orchestra conducted by Percy Pitt).

Recitative.

Giunse alfin il momento, che godrò senza affanno
in braccio all' idol mio.
Timide cure! uscite dal mio petto, a turbar non
venite il mio diletto!
Oh come par che all' amoroso foco l'amenità del
loco, la terra e il ciel risponda, come la notte
i furti miei seconda!

Aria. Deh, vieni, non tardar, o gioia bella,
Vieni ove amore per goder t' appella,
Finchè non splende in ciel notturna face,
Finchè l'aria è ancor bruna, e il mondo tace.
Quà mormora il ruscel, quì scherza l'aura,
Che col dolce susurro il cor ristaura,
Qui ridono i fioretti e l'erba é fresca,
Ai piaceri d'amor quì tutto adesca.
Vieni ben mio, tra queste piante ascose, vieni,
Ti vo' la fronte incoronar di rose.

FREE TRANSLATION.[1]

It is granted at last then without trembling
or danger, my lov'd one, I may meet thee.
Hence, idle terrors, all thought of fear has vanish'd,
from my bosom henceforth be ye banish'd.
Oh how the night, in still mysterious shadow,
seems to my longing fancy, to echo my fond emotion,
Come, let me tell thee thou hast my heart's devotion.

Oh come my heart's delight, where love invites thee,
Come then, for without thee no joy delights me,
The moon and stars for us have veiled their splendour,
Philomela has hush'd her carols tender.
The brooklet murmurs near with sound caressing,
'Tis the hour for love and love's confessing,
The zephyr o'er the flowers is softly playing,
Love's enchantment alone all things is swaying,
Come then my treasure, in silence all reposes,
Thy love is waiting to wreathe thy brow with roses.

[1] By Lady Macfarren, in Novello's edition of the Opera.

There is no need to recount the exact circumstances in which this is sung. It is to be enjoyed simply as a most beautiful vocal tune, with a very delightful light instrumental part, a feature of which lies in the brief **Wood-wind** interpolations between the vocal phrases.

As examples of these last, note that immediately following the vocal phrase given above comes a little three-note connexion between it and the next phrase, given to **Oboe** and **Bassoon.** The next two phrases are similarly followed, and then comes this longer interpolation:

Another delicious bit of **Wood-wind** (combined this time with **Plucked Strings**) is the one which ends the piece:

Large Vocalion Record. (On the reverse, *Voi lo sapete*, from Mascagni's *Cavalleria Rusticana.*) J. 04108, 4*s.* 6*d.*

Or,

Large H.M.V. Record. (On the reverse, *Quel guardo* from Donizetti's *Don Pasquale.*) DB. 567, 8*s.* 6*d.*

The orchestra is the better on the Vocalion Record. Perhaps Pareto has the better voice, judged by operatic standards, and sings more in the conventional Italian style, whilst Destournel has more feeling, more musical sensitiveness, and the more sympathetic voice. The Vocalion Record omits the Recitative.

Printed Music. *Figaro* is published by Novello at 5*s.* 6*d.* (paper) and 7*s.* 6*d.* (cloth). This song will also be found in Book II of same publisher's *Figaro Songs*, 2*s.*

Overture[1] . . . . *Figaro* . . . . Mozart

Mozart. *Overture to 'Figaro'.*

This is Mozart's Overture to his brilliant opera setting of a plot taken from Beaumarchais' play *Le Mariage de Figaro*, which also furnished Rossini with his plot for *The Barber of Seville.* It had its first performance in Vienna in 1786. (Characteristic of Mozart is the fact that the score is dated as completed on 29th April and that the performance took place on 1st May; the composition had, by the way, taken only six weeks.) The Irish tenor, Michael Kelly, took part, and records the enthusiasm of performers and audience:

> Even at the final rehearsal, all present were roused to enthusiasm; and when Benucci came to the fine passage 'Cherubina, alla vittoria, alla gloria militar', which he gave with stentorian lungs, the effect was electric. The whole of the performers on the stage and those in the orchestra vociferated 'Bravo! Bravo, Maestro! Viva, viva! Grande Mozart!'
>
> And Mozart. I shall never forget his little countenance when lighted up with the glowing rays of genius; it is impossible to describe it, as it would be to paint sunbeams.

The Overture is a brilliant, breathless piece of work. It begins *pianissimo*, with this scurrying theme on all the Strings, in octaves:

[1] For recordings of this Overture see p. 112.

At once followed by a delightfully contrasted Wood-wind passage:

This whole passage is then repeated, the scurrying Strings this time having added above them a more sedative Wood-wind (Flute and Oboe) counterpoint.

All so far constitutes the First Subject of the piece.

Some brilliant String-rushes follow, the rest of the orchestra punctuating them with interjectory chords. All this is a 'Bridge Passage', and it ends with a determined Mozartean cadence, making us feel that we are coming to the end of one section and about to begin another, which other is, of course, the 'Second Subject'. This opens rather plaintively yet happily; some delicate work by Oboes in thirds, answered by Flutes in thirds, also makes an important feature.

A later portion of the Second Subject is a pleasant little tune:

This is given out by First Violins, doubled an octave below

by Bassoon, and then doubled an octave higher by Flute, the Bassoon still doubling an octave below.

(Note the long-held Horn note about here.)

This ends the Exposition of the Overture. The Development (if indeed it can be called a Development) which follows is only a few bars long, and almost immediately, with the return of the Strings in the First Subject, we are rushed into the Recapitulation.

This requires no description.

A short Coda begins *pianissimo* with Strings alone; and gradually the other instruments join in, and it works up quickly to *fortissimo*. It includes two unintentional (very passing) references to the Hallelujah Chorus (which really come from the interjectory chords of the 'Bridge Passage' following the First Subject—see p. 110), and some brilliant String and Wood-wind headlong down-hill rushes.

There are at least seven recordings of the *Figaro* Overture, as follows:

Large Polydor Record. Orchestra of the State Opera, Dresden, conducted by Fritz Busch. 65861, 5*s*. 9*d*. On the reverse, Smetana's *The Bartered Bride* Overture.

Large Polydor Record. Orchestra of the State Opera, Berlin, conducted by Leo Blech. 65825, 5*s*. 9*d*. On the reverse, *German Dances*, by Mozart.

Large Polydor Record. Orchestra of the Württemberg National Theatre, Stuttgart, conducted by Fritz Busch. 65511, 5*s*. 9*d*. On the reverse, Theme and First Variation from Max Reger's Variations and Fugue on a Theme by Mozart (Op. 132).

Large H.M.V. Record. Royal Albert Hall Orchestra, conducted by Sir Landon Ronald. D. 1005, 6*s*. 6*d*. On the reverse, Minuet and Trio from Mozart's Divertimento in D (K. 334). (This is perhaps the most popular of all Mozart's Minuets, being often heard as a detached piece.)

Large Parlophone Record. Opera House Orchestra, conducted by Edward Moerike. E. 10111, 4*s*. 6*d*. On the reverse, *Lichtertänze*, from Rubinstein's *Feramors*, played by the Michailow Orchestra.

Large Columbia Record. The Beecham Symphony Orchestra, conducted by Sir Thomas Beecham. L. 1115, 6*s*. 6*d*. On the reverse, Smetana's *The Bartered Bride* Overture.

Large Vocalion Record. The Aeolian Orchestra, conducted by Percy Fletcher. D. 02122, 4*s*. 6*d*. On the reverse Dvořák's *Slavonic Dance*, No. 3.

There is little to choose between these seven different recordings. This is probably a difficult piece to record; at any rate, none of these records is first-rate.

Polydor No. 65861 is placed first as it seems rather better than any of the others. In particular, it gives a delicious true *pianissimo* at the opening. But out of the other six, perhaps out of all seven, one may well choose that which attracts most by the piece on the reverse side of the disc.

The merry Overture to the Opera of Bohemian peasant life, *The Bartered Bride*, is a typical (and probably the best-known) example of the music of one of the first 'nationalist' composers. It well stands the cutting that it here receives—though Columbia is very drastic.

The *German Dances* furnish a good example of the lightest of all Mozart's light music. Mozart wrote an immense quantity of dance-music, which it is interesting to compare with that of our own times.

The Theme of Reger's Variations is the Air on which Mozart himself wrote Variations for the First Movement of his Piano Sonata in A (K. 331—the 'Op. 132' applies to Reger's Variations, not to Mozart's Theme).

Rubinstein's *Lichtertänze* has more value in pretty orchestral colour than in musical quality.

Dvořák's *Slavonic Dance* adds attractive orchestral colour to simple, exhilarating music.

Printed Music. Miniature Full Score of the *Figaro* Overture, Goodwin & Tabb, 1*s*. 6*d*. Arrangements for Piano Solo or Piano Duet can also be obtained.

RECORD No. 39

Vocal Solo . . . *In uomini, in soldati* . . . . Mozart

(From the Opera *Così fan tutte.*)

LUCREZIA BORI.

In uomini, in soldati,
Sperare fedeltà?
Non vi fate sentir per carità!
Di pasta simile son tutti quanti,
Son tutti quanti le fronde mobili,
L'aure inconstanti han' più degli uomini stabilità.
Mentite lagrime, fallaci sguardi,
Voci ingannevoli, vezzi bugiardi
Son le primarie lor qualità.
In noi non amano che il lor diletto;
Poi ci dispregiano, negano l'affetto,
Nè val da' barbari chieder pietà.
Paghiam, o femine, d'ugual moneta
Questa malefica razza indiscreta;
Amiam per comodo, per vanità.
La ra la.

FREE TRANSLATION.

In men and in soldiers
What faith can be placed?
For all are alike, and none of them chaste,
They are all of them baked of the very same paste.

The leaf on the tree, the breeze in the air,
Are as stable as men—and have something to spare.
Man's tears they are truthless, his looks are a lie.
His voice is beguiling, his manners are sly.
And you he loves merely for what you can give,
That got, he is happy and without you can live.
Never humble yourself by asking for grace,
Just pay tit-for-tat, and preserve a smooth face.

This is not, of course, a singing translation, but it gives the sense, I think. I take responsibility for that, but not for the ethical principle advocated.

This sparkling little air from Mozart's *Così fan tutte* (literal translation—'Thus do they all') is sung by the maid-servant, Despina, in circumstances that will be clear from the following description of the plot, taken, for its admirable concision, from Mr. E. J. Dent's *Mozart's Operas—A Critical Study* (Chatto & Windus):

'The plot of the opera is simplicity itself. Ferrando and Guglielmo are two young Neapolitan officers engaged to be married to two young ladies, Fiordiligi and her sister Dorabella. A cynical old bachelor, Don Alfonso by name, persuades the young men to put their mistresses' constancy to the test. They pretend to be called away from Naples on duty, but return that very afternoon disguised as Albanian noblemen. Don Alfonso, with the help of Despina, the ladies' maid, persuades the two sisters to receive them. The strangers make violent love to them, and after some opposition each succeeds in winning the heart of his friend's betrothed. The affair proceeds, in fact, with such rapidity that a notary is called in that very evening to witness the marriage contract. Suddenly Don Alfonso announces the return of the soldiers; the Albanians vanish, and the terrified ladies are obliged to make confession to their original lovers. It is needless to say, however, that all ends happily.'

Save for a bar or two's interruption of a recitative character (just after the laugh) this is just a lovely, continuous tune in which some phrases are purely instrumental, and others joined in by the voice. Nothing more gay and *insouciant* can be imagined.

The singer does her part with humour and sprightliness. The slight hardness in her voice may be greatly mitigated by a trifling decrease in the speed at which the gramophone is set.

Small H.M.V. Record. DA. 132, 6*s*. (On the reverse Mascagni's *In pure stille*, from *Iris*.)

Printed Music. The Opera is published by Novello, at 7*s*. 6*d*. (paper) and 11*s*. 6*d*. (cloth).

RECORDS Nos. 40, 41, 42, AND 43

Violin and Pianoforte Duet *The 'Kreutzer' Sonata* . . Beethoven
ISOLDE MENGES AND ARTHUR DE GREEF.

Kreutzer was a French violinist of standing. The Sonata was first played by Beethoven himself and Bridgetower, a mulatto violinist, at a concert in Vienna in 1803. But it was not dedicated to Bridgetower, perhaps because (if Beethoven's friend, Ries, is to be trusted) Beethoven and he quarrelled about a girl.

As a specimen of Beethoven's correspondence may not be unwelcome, here is a letter from him to his publisher Simrock, about this Sonata:

Vienna, October 4, 1804.

Dear, best Herr Simrock, I have been all the time waiting anxiously for my Sonata which I gave you—but in vain. Do please write and tell me the reason of the delay—whether you have taken it from me merely to give it as food to the moths? or do you wish to claim it by special imperial privilege? Well, I thought that might have happened long ago. This slow devil who was to beat out this Sonata, where is he hiding? As a rule you are a quick devil; it is known that, like Faust, you are in league with the black one, and on that very account *so beloved* by your comrades. Once again—where is your devil—or what kind of a devil is it—who is sitting on my Sonata, and with whom you are at loggerheads? So hurry up and tell me when I shall see the Sonata brought to the light of day. If you will fix the time, I will at once send you a little note to Kreutzer, which be kind enough to enclose when you are sending a *copy* (as anyhow you will send copies to Paris, or will have them printed there). This Kreutzer is a good, amiable man, who during his stay here gave me much pleasure. His unaffectedness and natural manner are more to my taste than all the *extérieur* or *intérieur* of most *virtuosi*. As the Sonata is written for a first-rate player, the dedication to him is all the more fitting. Although we are in correspondence with each other (i. e., I write once every year), I hope he will know nothing about it as yet. I constantly hear that your prosperity rests on a basis which is ever becoming more and more sound; I am heartily glad at this. Greetings to all your family, and to all whom you think will be pleased to receive a greeting from me. An answer soon, please.

BEETHOVEN.[1]

[1] From *The Letters of Ludwig van Beethoven* (J. M. Dent & Co.).

The Sonata consists of an Introduction and Three Movements:

Adagio sostenuto (= Slow and sustained),
Presto (= Quick),
Andante con Variazioni (=A rather slow air with variations),
Finale—Presto (=Quick).

The Introduction opens with Violin alone:

Then the Piano takes up the theme. As the Introduction ends and the Presto begins, note how the First Subject of the latter grows out of the ending of the former. (The tail of one and head of the other are shown below.)

This First Subject is short and concentrated. Piano repeats it, and it is very briefly developed. Then follows a long agitated passage of rushing arpeggios and flashing chords. The simple but deep Second Subject is a fine contrast to the First:

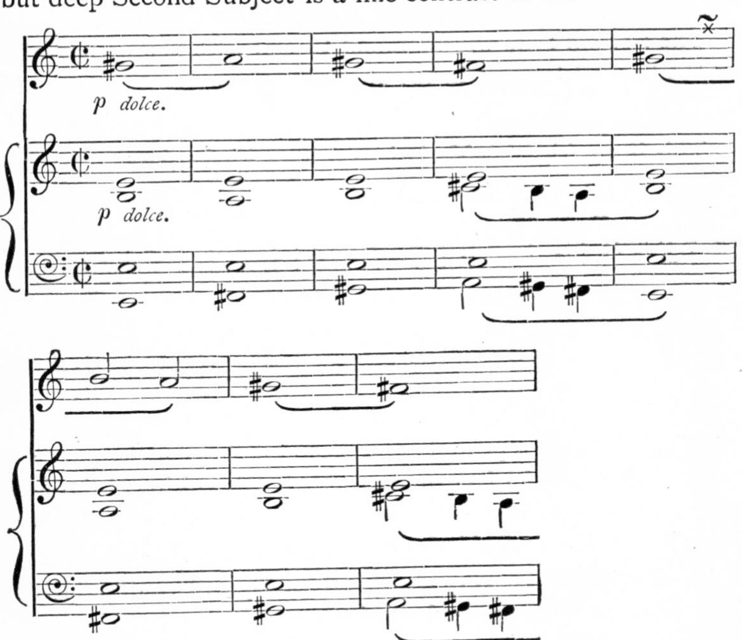

It is followed by more rushing arpeggios and a Third, fiery, leaping Tune.

You will notice that its little two-note figure is really that of the First Subject:

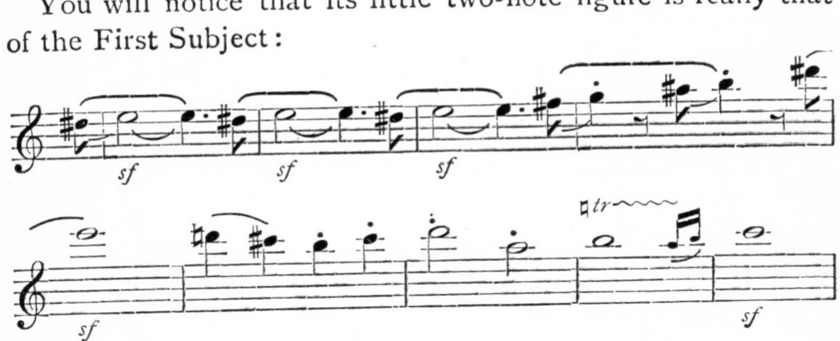

The long Development Section (which begins on Side Two) is almost entirely taken up with this Third Tune.

The driving forcefulness of the Movement is hardly for a moment allowed to subside, and when at length the Recapitulation comes, everything is extended and intensified.

The Second Side will be found to end with the appearance of the Second Subject in the Recapitulation.

Second Movement.

This is an Air with Variations. The Air begins:

It is in the familiar 'Ternary' Form. There are two parts, each of which is repeated; the second is twice as long as the first and includes for its own second half a repetition of the first part. The Piano begins the second part alone, but the Violin joins in for the last half of this second part.

The Variations are very clear, and hardly call for description. This Movement is a very favourite one.

In each of Variations 1–3 the second part is not repeated in this performance.

Third Movement.

Like the First Movement, this is in Sonata Form.

The First Subject opens in two-part counterpoint:

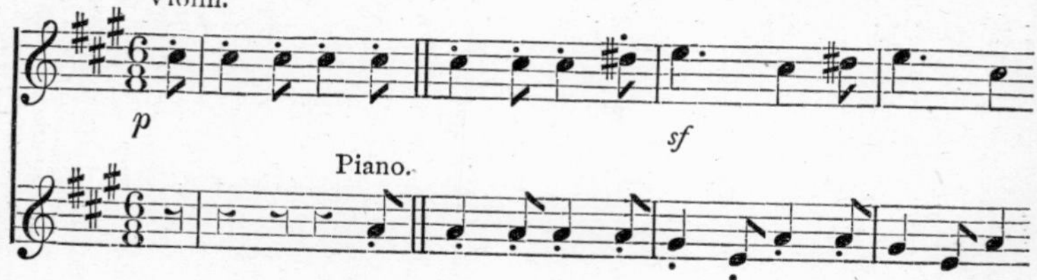

Immediately afterwards the two parts are heard reversed—the piano now above the violin :

The Second Subject is in two parts—a flippant tune and a poetical one. The flippant one (Violin, with mere accompaniment in Piano) is nearly related to the First Subject :

By and by this is given to the Piano, the Violin amusing itself in acrobatics meanwhile.

Here is the contrasting poetical subject :

The treatment of this is very loving. It forms a most effective passage of contrast in an almost entirely brilliant Movement.

But very soon the general mood of excitement reasserts itself and the poetical Theme is forgotten. (The Record turns over at the end of the Enunciation.)

There is practically nothing to be said of the Development Section and the Recapitulation. The Development Section is comparatively short.

When the First Subject returns, its original bare two-part-counterpoint is filled out, with increasing excitement.

Though the Movement is in proportion to the colossal scale of the whole Sonata, yet everything is absolutely simple and direct.

The whole work is a magnificent example of Beethoven's fiery, even ferocious temperament.

This is a splendid performance, except that de Greef is inclined to be hard and unsympathetic, notably in the Air of the Second Movement; and it is a splendid recording, except that the tone of the Violin is given that shrillness we so often find on the latest Records.

Four Large H.M.V. Records. D. 1066–9, each 6*s.* 6*d.* Published complete in Album.

There is also a **Polydor** recording (Robert Zeiler and Bruno Seidler-Winkler: four large Records, 65760–3, each 5*s.* 9*d.*), but unfortunately the recording is not good, and the Violinist (Zeiler) has not here the splendid strength of Isolde Menges. There are three points in Polydor's favour: the interpretation is, perhaps, very slightly better; the Pianist has not the hardness of, and is altogether more sensitive than, de Greef; and the Violin tone has not the shrillness of the H.M.V. Records.

The turn-overs on the Polydor Records either explain themselves, or are the same as those on the H.M.V. Records, except in the Last Movement, where Polydor includes the Development Section on the First Side.

Printed Music. The Beethoven Violin and Piano Sonatas may be got in various editions, e. g. Augener (edited by Kreisler), 12*s.* The single Sonata may also be had, price 2*s.* 6*d.* Miniature Score, Goodwin & Tabb, 1*s.* 6*d.*

RECORDS Nos. 44, 45, AND 46

String Quartet . . *Quartet in G*, Op. 18, No. 2 . . Beethoven

THE CATTERALL QUARTET.

This is an early Quartet composed in 1801, when Beethoven was thirty-one. It is spring-like and fresh.

The Movements are:

1. Allegro (= Bright and quick),
2. Adagio cantabile; Allegro; Adagio cantabile (= Slow and singing; Quick; Slow and singing),
3. Scherzo, Allegro (= Bright and quick),
4. Allegro molto quasi presto (= Very quick).

First Movement.

This Movement is in 'First-Movement', or 'Sonata Form', and therefore consists of an Enunciation of the subject-matter, a Development of it, and a Recapitulation of it, with a Coda.

The First Subject is quietly happy:

(By the way—surely the popular Praeludium of Järnefeldt owes a little to the fifth and sixth bars of this.)

The Second Subject has a slightly more thoughtful tinge.

Florid passages, in which the beat is divided by scales or arabesques into sextolets or octuplets (such passages being most often, but by no means exclusively given to the First Violin) are a feature of the movement. The First Violin has in some places almost a Concerto-like independence, and it often soars high. The Enunciation is repeated in full, occupying the First Side of the Record. In the Recapitulation the decorative turn in eighth-of-a-beat notes in the First Subject is passed from hand to hand with happy effect.

Everything is delicately done, the harmonies are peculiarly gracious, and the Movement is really a model of light-handed refinement. The ending with a reference to the 'Praeludium' theme, by First Violin, followed by the same theme in Viola, accompanied by *pizzicato* chords, is grace itself.

Second Movement.

This is a song-like slow movement, with an interpolation of a fanciful, almost freakish quick section.

The opening theme begins:

The quick middle section is fashioned out of this *motif* (stolen from the end of the slow section just completed):

There are two 'repeat' marks which are not observed, so that in this performance this middle section seems rather unduly short.

When the slow first section returns, the air of the theme just shown is at the opening given to 'Cello instead of to First Violin.

Third Movement.

This is a Scherzo (and so entitled) with a Trio, and then the return of the Scherzo.

The spirit of the Movement is very Haydnish.

The Trio pretends to be rather solemn:

The spirit of this Trio is that of Dr. Johnson's friend who had tried to be a philosopher, 'but, I don't know how, cheerfulness was always breaking in'.

The cheerfulness takes the form of a jump with a chirpy trill and some triplets. The voice of conscience on a low G tries to check levity, but fails completely, and the gaiety of the Trio is soon almost as well established as that of the Scherzo proper.

Fourth Movement.

This is in Sonata Form. It is, again, rather skittishly Haydn-like.

The First Subject opens in the 'Cello:

This is then taken up and responded to by all the instruments.

Then the 'Cello speaks again, and again the crowd responds, Great play is made with this theme, and at one point you will hear it forcibly played by 'Cello, whilst the other instruments are busy with other things above it.

Soon after this passage the Second Subject enters in the two Violins:

Note the skilful and happy way in which these twin themes are given to the various instruments.

The Enunciation section continues for some time after this.

The Development opens with a quotation of the early part of the First Subject, transposed into a remote key—rather unexpected in effect. At the end of the Development is another Modulation of similar effect.

The opening of the Recapitulation, just after this, cannot possibly be missed. In it there is much agile elaboration, all of which, however, explains itself when one knows the material of the Movement.

The turn-over of the Record comes half-way through the Development Section.

Three Large H.M.V. Records. D. 997–9, each 6*s.* 6*d.*
Printed Music. Miniature Score, Goodwin & Tabb, 1*s.* 6*d.*

RECORD No. 47

Song . . . . . *In questa tomba oscura* . . . Beethoven

CHALIAPIN.

The curious origin of this very popular but extremely doleful composition is given by Thayer, Beethoven's biographer, in a quotation from the *Journal des Luxus* (November 1806):

'A bit of musical pleasantry recently gave rise to a competition amongst a number of famous composers. Countess Rzewuska improvised an aria at the pianoforte; the poet Carpani at once improvised a text for it. He imagined a lover who had died of grief because of the indifference of his lady-love; she, repenting of her hard-heartedness, bedews the grave; and now the shade calls to her:

In questa tomba oscura
Lasciami riposar;
Quando vivevo, ingrata,
Dovevi a me pensar.

Lascia che l'ombre ignude
Godansi pace almen,
E non bagnar mie ceneri
D'inutile velen.

These words have been set by Paër, Salieri, Weigl, Zingarelli, Cherubini, Asioli, and other great masters and amateurs. Zingarelli alone provided ten compositions of them; in all about fifty have been collected and the poet purposes to give them to the public in a volume.'

Thayer adds:

'The number of compositions was increased to sixty-three, and they were published in 1808, the last (No. 63) being by Beethoven. This was by no means considered the best at the time, although it alone now survives.'

The Carpani mentioned was apparently popular in Vienna musical circles. It was he who wrote the Italian text of Haydn's *The Creation*, for performance on Haydn's 76th birthday, upon which occasion 'Beethoven was one of those who, "with members of high nobility", stood at the door of the hall of the university to receive the venerable guest on his arrival there in Prince Esterhazy's coach, and who accompanied him as "sitting in an armchair he was carried, lifted high, and on his entrance into the hall was received with the sound of trumpets and drums by the numerous gathering and greeted with joyous shouts of 'Long live Haydn!'"'

As Beethoven left *In questa tomba* it had but pianoforte accompaniment; here it is sung (sometimes a trifle sharp, by the way—but we pardon a lot in Chaliapin!) to orchestral accompaniment.

TRANSLATION.[1]

This lowly tomb my refuge,
To rest, O, leave me free!
Yet while I lived—ungrateful!
Thou shouldst have thought on me.
Peace to my weary spirit
Let these lone shades endear,
No more, at least, contemn,
Nor shed thy tears deceitful here.

Large H.M.V. Record. DB. 107, 8*s*. 6*d*. (On the reverse, Rossini's *La Calunnia è un venticello* from *The Barber of Seville*.)

Printed Music. Volumes of Beethoven's Songs published by various firms. This particular song is also published separately by Joseph Williams, 1*s*. 6*d*. (Two editions, one with Italian and English words, the other with Italian words only; apart from this the editions are identical.) It is also published by Augener (with Italian, English and German words—the Italian is the original).

[1] By W. Ball, from Messrs. Augener's edition of the song.

Symphony No. 5, in C minor . . . . Beethoven

THE ROYAL ALBERT HALL ORCHESTRA.
(Conducted by Sir Landon Ronald.)

The recording in full of Beethoven's most popular (and in many respects, finest) symphony is indeed a boon, and one rejoices that at last every one of his nine Symphonies is similarly available for home study.[1]

The best way of becoming thoroughly acquainted with this great work is to go carefully through the Records again and again, with either the orchestral score or a piano 'arrangement', or (not at all a bad plan) first with the piano 'arrangement' and then with orchestral score.

A detailed book on Beethoven's Symphonies, and one which is valuable not only for the biographical, historical, and technical particulars it supplies, but also for the enthusiasm it communicates, is the late Sir George Grove's *Beethoven and his Nine Symphonies* (Novello, 9*s*. net). The description which here follows will, however, probably be thought sufficient by many Gramophonists.

The Symphony was composed at intervals from 1805 to 1808, when Beethoven was 35 to 38 years of age. It represents a very great advance in many ways upon his previous symphonies.

A close examination of the Symphony will reveal to the student, perhaps to his surprise, the small amount of material out of which a great work can be constructed.

The score of this Symphony contains 1,565 bars (not counting the many 'repeats'). Yet the whole material out of which it is organized amounts, on a careful computation, to under 35 bars.

First Movement.

Of the economy of the composer the First Movement offers an especially striking example. Its 502 bars are entirely

[1] All Beethoven's Symphonies are now issued by the Parlophone and Polydor Companies, and some besides the Fifth by some English Companies.

constructed from the material contained in six bars of its early pages, the rhythmic call to attention with which it opens:

and the flowing melody which afterwards creeps in:

Out of the first of these little *motifs* the whole of the First Subject is evolved, in this sort of way:[1]

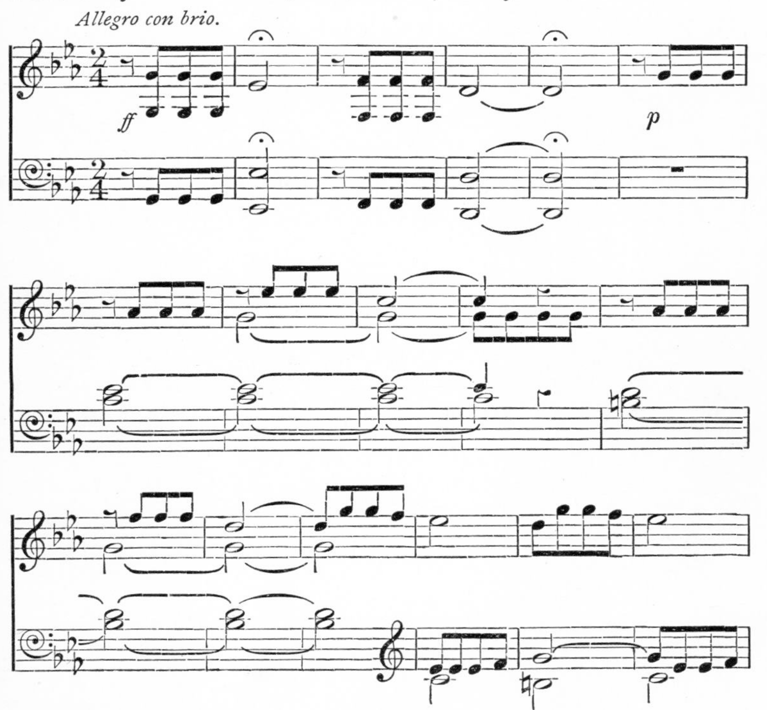

[1] The extracts here given in pianoforte 'arrangement' are from the edition by E. Pauer, published by Messrs. Augener & Co., mentioned under 'Printed Music' (on p. 144).

Out of the second little *motif* the whole Second Subject is evolved, a pervading touch of the first *motif* being also ever present in the bass :

The First Movement of this Symphony (as of most of the Sonatas and Symphonies of the classical period) is in what we call 'Sonata Form' or 'First Movement Form', i.e. it consists of:

(*a*) A section (technically called the **Enunciation**) giving the subject-matter as above, and coming to a sort of semicolon or colon, after which the section is generally repeated.

(*b*) A section (technically called the **Development**) in which this subject-matter is 'developed', i.e. treated in a variety of interesting ways in a variety of keys.

(*c*) A section (technically called the **Recapitulation**) which is almost a duplicate of section (*a*) save that the two Subjects, which were in different keys before, have now the same key-note, and that a good long 'Coda' or tail-piece is added to make an effective ending.

It seems better to call this 'First-Movement Form', for 'Sonata Form' should surely denote the form of a *whole work* in the Sonata class.

Try first Section I (the **Enunciation**) which (when it has been repeated) takes you about two-thirds through the first side of the first Record. Go through it several times, and listen keenly to the matter and the composer's treatment of it. If you are inclined to think that any passage introduces matter other than what is evolved from the two little *motifs* mentioned, listen again keenly, and you will find that you are wrong.

Little need be told you about the orchestration of this section. The strings are the dominant factor, but there are some lovely wood-wind bits—see the names of instruments that have been inserted in the Second Subject as given above, and note also that the Second Subject is introduced by a bold Horn call, made from the first *motif*:

Now proceed to the Second Section (the **Development**), which opens:

Notice one famous passage where first alternate two-chords, and then alternate one-chords, are given to Wood-wind and Strings, in a sort of echo. This, with the harmonies chosen, produces an effect of expectancy, and, as a matter of fact, is (considered formally) intended to draw the attention of our (conscious or subconscious) mind to the beginning of the Third Section.

This Third Section (or **Recapitulation**) opens as did the First Section, save that the initial call is now given to the Full Orchestra in all its violence (Strings, Wood-wind, Horns, Trumpets, and Timpani). Immediately after this call this side of the Record ends, and we have to turn over—a rather unfortunate break.

In his treatment of the First-Subject material this time, Beethoven has introduced a very effective and beautiful Oboe *cadenza*, providing an entrancing moment of repose:

Then he proceeds, and shortly afterwards we have the Second Subject, ushered in as before.

Much of the Coda is strenuous; emotionally this is, perhaps, the climax of the Movement.

Now go a good many times through this Movement, learning to recognize all its beauties, and becoming as familiar with it as you are with your favourite poem or novel.

Second Movement.

This is a very lovely slow Air with Variations, or rather, as we may say, if we like, 'Double Air with Double Variations', for we may regard it as made out of two tunes.

The first tune begins thus:

And its Variations begin in these several ways:

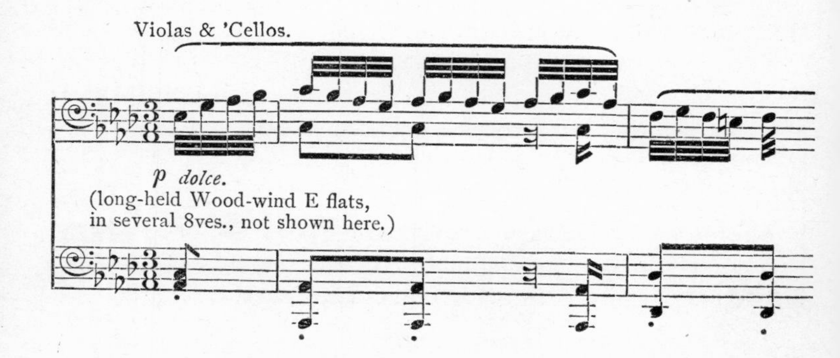

Sandwiched in with these varying treatments of the First Air is a Second Air, in varying treatments:

(Beethoven has simply taken over this double-air-double-variation idea, lock, stock, and barrel, from Haydn—see the slow movement of Haydn's first symphony of the well-known set of twelve.)

Orchestrally a good deal of the interest of this lovely Movement lies in certain passages for Wood-wind alone, and also certain passages where some tiny touch of a Flute or other Wood-wind instrument has been added above a theme. The Trumpets and Horns, where they enter, as they several times do on one of the appearances of Air II, are impressive. This is a Movement that will pay for studying with the Orchestral score.

The Record turns over in the middle of the Movement. Immediately after the turn is a beautiful passage of scaly-bits, in Flute and Oboe, with two Clarinets playing simultaneously similar scaly-bits always in the contrary direction.

The Bassoon has a bit of Air I as an effective little solo about 1¼ inches before the end of the Record.

Pursuing our idea of 'economy' in composition, it will be found on examination that the whole of this 247-bar Movement is wrought out of two *motifs* of a couple of bars apiece.

Third Movement.

This (though not so called) is a Scherzo, and one of Beethoven's most daring efforts in this direction. It is a wonderful combination of mysticism and humour.

Its various germs are as follows:

(This has an obvious relation to the First Subject of the First Movement.)

Berlioz likened this to 'the gambols of an elephant': he ought to have said to a small herd of elephants, since it is for the most part fugally treated, one section of the String force after another taking it up.

The Movement falls into three clear parts:

(*a*) The Scherzo proper, made from the first two of the themes given above.

(*b*) The 'Trio', made from the third of the themes given above.

(*c*) The Scherzo, proper, again.

Interesting orchestral features are:

1. The frequent use of the Bass Strings alone, producing usually a very mysterious effect, but sometimes a half-comic one.

2. A lovely long high holding-note for Oboe about $\frac{3}{4}$ inch from the outer edge of first side of Record.

3. A beautiful passage for Wood-wind alone, about $\frac{1}{2}$ inch from end of first side of Record: the solo Flute has the tune high up, and the Oboes, Clarinets, and Bassoons accompany it with slow chords. As this brief passage ends it comes down an arpeggio step-ladder, carried first for a few steps by Flute, then a few by Oboe, then a few more by Clarinet and Bassoon. (Play a passage like this many times and learn to recognize and delight in the contrasts of tone colour.) This passage is immediately followed by:

4. *Pizzicato* notes in 'Cellos and Double-basses.

5. The First Theme treated as before.

6. Four bars of harmony by Clarinets, Bassoons, and Horns.

7. The First Theme very humorously, yet delicately, treated by solo Bassoon *staccato*, with 'Cellos *pizzicato*, answered by other Strings *pizzicato* (here the first side of the Record ends).

8. (Beginning of other side of Record.) The Second Theme is taken for 4 bars by Clarinet (with soft String accompaniment) and then for 4 bars by First Violins *pizzicato*, then for 4 bars by Oboe, then by First Violins *pizzicato* again.

9. Almost immediately after this the Bassoon has some delicate bits (in which, on the H.M.V. Record, he sounds exactly like a Banjo!). At first it alternates (in a little 2-note *motif*) with the Violins *pizzicato*, and then it follows this by taking up the First Theme *staccato* in unison with the 'Cellos *pizzicato* as it did once before—see (7) above.

10. A lot of effective soft *pizzicato* String work follows, and then comes a remarkable passage,[1] which has been thus

[1] Compare Beethoven's so-called 'Harp' Quartet (Op. 74) at exactly the same place.

eloquently described by Parry: 'The whole of the *Scherzo* of the C minor Symphony is as near being miraculous as a human work can be; but one of its most absorbing moments is the part where, for fifteen bars, there is nothing going on but an insignificant chord continuously held by low strings and a *pianissimo* rhythmic beat of the drum. Taken out of its context it would be perfectly meaningless. As Beethoven has used it, it is infinitely more impressive than the greatest noise Meyerbeer and his followers ever succeeded in making.'

Fourth Movement.

The allusion to the 'greatest noises' of music just quoted has an illustration at once, for the passage described passes (about 1¼ inches from outer edge of Record) straight into the following, with all the force of the Full Orchestra, with 3 Trombones, Double-Bassoon and Piccolo now added:

In some churches in small towns on the Continent, if you attend Mass on Corpus Christi day you will at the end hear the Blessing solemnly pronounced, and then, without a pause, the West doors are flung open, a brass band outside strikes up a rowdy march, and the congregation crowds out for dancing and jollity. The contrast is startling, and the transition here has much the same effect.

The last Movement is exhilarating, but in pure musical value most people would probably class it well below the three preceding Movements.

This Movement, like the First, is in 'Sonata Form'. Its First Subject is the theme just quoted, its Second Subject falls into two parts, beginning as follows:

The treatment of these, in Enunciation, Development, and Recapitulation, is pretty normal, but note that with fine effect, immediately before the Recapitulation, a passage from the Scherzo is inserted, obviously in order to get the blessing-brass-band contrast once again, on the re-entry of the rowdy chief theme.

Towards the very end, as a part of the Coda, note how this brass-band theme is treated in canon, the Brass and Wood giving it out, overlapped (at a bar's distance) by the String Basses.

The change to the new Record occurs between the Enunciation and Development. One or two orchestral points to note are:

(1) In the inserted allusion to the Scherzo, a lovely long holding-note by Oboe.

(2) Nearly $1\frac{1}{2}$ inches from outer rim of last side of Record, a sort of hunting call:

first by Bassoons, then by Horns, then taken up and reiterated by more and more instruments—Flute, Clarinet, Bassoon, Oboe, and Piccolo (the Oboe is difficult to catch here), and afterwards by Strings.

(3) Shortly after this comes a long Piccolo shake. From this point onwards the music is nothing better than a 'jolly good row', and the village brass-band ending is rather cheap. But by this time everybody is thoroughly worked up and it will pass!

Four large H.M.V. Records. D. 665-6-7-8, each 6*s.* 6*d.*

Parlophone have also recorded this Symphony (Berlin State Opera House Orchestra, conducted by Dr. Weissmann—four large Records, E. 10284-7, each 4*s.* 6*d.*, issued complete in Album), also **Columbia** (Weingartner and the London Symphony Orchestra—four large Records, L. 1640-3, each 6*s.* 6*d.*, issued complete in Album with descriptive notes).

The H.M.V. Records were alone in their glory when this book first appeared, and are still, perhaps, the best all round. The playing is almost flawless, and the recording very fine and satisfying. Parlophone are superior on the interpretative side all through, but their recording is distinctly inferior, except in some of the Finale. Columbia are well recorded, and are excellent dynamically (H.M.V. underdo their *pp*, *p*, and *ff*) but unfortunately show a great deal of unsteadiness, raggedness and faulty intonation, so that their Records are probably the worst of the three issues.

Details in the above description apply to the H.M.V. Records. Changes of Record for Parlophone and Columbia which differ from H.M.V. are given below. Beyond this, any one who chooses the Parlophone or Columbia recording will, I think, find it easy to adapt for them the details of my description.

In the First Movement, Parlophone does not repeat the Enunciation, and Columbia turns over half-way through the Development Section. In the Second Movement Parlophone turns over shortly before my third music quotation, and again just before the fifth. Columbia has the whole of the Scherzo and Finale labelled as 'Finale'. On these two Columbia Records fresh sides begin, one at (7) in my description, next with the second part of the Second Subject (see p. 142), and the last soon after the beginning of the Recapitulation. Parlophone's first turn-over comes with the 'remarkable passage' described under (10), the second with the return in the Finale of part of the Scherzo.

In the Scherzo, Parlophone does not repeat the first section of the Trio, and in the Finale none of the Records repeats the Enunciation.

Polydor have also recorded this Symphony (four large Records, 69638–41, 5*s*. 9*d*. each), but I have unfortunately not been able to hear these Records.

Printed Music. Miniature orchestral score, Goodwin & Tabb, 4*s*. Pianoforte Solo copy, Augener, No. 8036 e, 3*s*. (or the whole set of first five Symphonies, No. 8006 a, 7*s*.); Pianoforte Duet copy, Augener, No. 8517 e, 2*s*. 6*d*. (or the whole set of first five, No. 8516 a, 6*s*. 6*d*.).

RECORD No. 52

Song . . . . . *Wohin?*[1] . . . . . Schubert

Ich hört' ein Bächlein rauschen
Wohl aus dem Felsenquell,
Hinab zum Tale rauschen
So frisch und wunderhell.

Ich weiss nicht, wie mir wurde,
Nicht, wer den Rat mir gab,
Ich musste auch hinunter
Mit meinem Wanderstab.

Hinunter und immer weiter,
Und immer dem Bache nach,
Und immer frischer rauschte
Und immer heller der Bach.

Ist das denn meine Strasse?
O Bächlein, sprich, wohin?
Du hast mit deinem Rauschen
Mir ganz berauscht den Sinn.

Was sag' ich denn vom Rauschen?
Das kann kein Rauschen sein:
Es singen wohl die Nixen
Tief unten ihren Reihn.

Lass singen, Gesell, lass rauschen,
Und wandre fröhlich nach!
Es gehn ja Mühlenräder
In jedem klaren Bach.

WHITHER?[2]

I heard a streamlet gushing
From out its rocky bed,
Far down the valley rushing,
So fresh and clear it sped.

[1] For singers see p. 148.

[2] The translation, which Olga Haley sings, by Maria X. Hayes, in Kappey's edition of *Sixty Songs by Schubert* (Boosey).

I know not why I pondered,
Nor whence the thought did flow,
E'en as he hastens downward
With my staff I too must go.

Still onward, but ever downward,
And ever still by the stream;
Which with refreshing murmur,
More bright and clear did gleam.

Must this then be my pathway?
O streamlet, tell me where
My path shall I find!
Thou hast with thy sweet murmur,
Bewildered quite my mind.

Why speak I of a murmur,
No murmur can it be.
The Nixies they are singing
'Neath the wave their melody.

Cease singing, my friends, cease murmuring,
And blithely wander near,
I hear the sound of millwheels
In every streamlet clear.

Wohin? is one of the songs of the famous *Die schöne Müllerin* ('The Beautiful Miller-woman') song-cycle, a setting of twenty poems from Wilhelm Müller's 'Müllerlieder' (or 'Mill Songs'). The cycle was composed in the year 1823.

The Schubert-Müller combination has prompted these

words from another of the Müller name, the late Prof. Max Müller, of Oxford, son of the poet himself:

'In olden days, Poetry and Music were inseparable. The Poet was also a Singer, and he produced neither Songs without Words, nor Words without Songs.

'Those times have long ago passed away, but their memory remains, and in the high moments of poetic inspiration Poetry yearns for the wings of song, Music struggles towards the liberating word.

'In modern days when the highest expression in either art without division of labour has become almost unattainable, yet the old good fortune holds sway when two such artists, as poet and musician, as Wilhelm Müller and Franz Schubert discover and understand one another. Here two souls are merged into one, and it seems to us to be almost as difficult to imagine *Die schöne Müllerin* and *Die Winterreise* without the Schubert melodies as to sing the Schubert songs without words. The songs of Wilhelm Müller, like all true songs of the people ['Volkslieder'], cry out for music, and what they in themselves lack is, we may almost say, more completely supplied in the music to which they are set than has been the case with the work of any poet of the nineteenth century.[1]

The story of the composition of this cycle is as follows: Schubert, calling at the house of his friend and brother composer, Randhartinger, found lying on the table a volume of Müller's poems, which Randhartinger himself intended to set. He put the volume in his pocket, and, arriving home in the early evening, began work at once on his settings. When Randhartinger called to see him next morning, he was surprised to find his book in Schubert's possession. 'Don't be angry with me,' said Schubert. 'The poems so took hold of me that I *had* to set them. I scarcely had a couple of hours' sleep last night, and here are seven of the poems already set. Try them over; I do hope you'll like them.'

Randhartinger, who was a good tenor singer, went through the seven songs. 'I will never touch the book again,' he said; 'after Schubert, Randhartinger has no right to compose.'

[1] Translated from Max Müller's introduction to the Peters *Schubert-Album*, vol. i.

Schubert completed his settings of these poems during the next few months, being occupied in the meantime with an Opera. Some of the songs were composed in hospital.

Large Parlophone Record. Emmy Bettendorf. E. 10388, 4*s.* 6*d.* On the same record, Schubert's *Haidenröslein* (*The Wild Rose*) and *Was ist Sylvia ?*.

Small H.M.V. Record. Elena Gerhardt. DA. 706, 6*s.* On the reverse, Schubert's *Das Lied im Grünen.*

Small Polydor Record. Leo Slezak. 62420, 4*s.* 6*d.* On the reverse, *Flieh, O flieh*' from Massenet's *Manon*, with orchestra.

In English—**Small Vocalion Record.** Olga Haley, accompanied by Ivor Newton. R. 6143, 3*s.* On the reverse, Duparc's *Chanson Triste.*

Of the three recordings in German given, each is good enough if one specially wishes to choose according to the other songs on the records. Emmy Bettendorf's is quite the best, and has with *Wohin ?* two more of Schubert's loveliest Songs (perhaps in *Who is Sylvia ?* the loveliest of all) very beautifully sung. Slezak is perhaps rather too 'soulful'.

Olga Haley sings *Wohin ?* very delightfully in English, and a good modern French song in French.

Printed Music. This song will be found in many volumes of Schubert's songs. The Boosey Volume (5*s.*), which gives the English translation sung by Olga Haley, also gives the German text, and contains *The Wild Rose*, *Who is Sylvia ?*, and *The Erl-King* and *Serenade* (see p. 164). A copy (with English words) can be obtained for 3*d.* in Novello's School-Songs (No. 670).

The 'Unfinished' Symphony . . . . Schubert
(Parlophone, Polydor, and H.M.V.)[1]

This Symphony was written in 1822, when the composer was twenty-five years old. He wrote the two movements here recorded, and nine bars of a third one, probably giving a week or ten days to the task, and then, so far as we know, never touched it again during the six years he had still to live. The work remained in manuscript and quite unknown for forty years after the composer was in his grave, and was then published at Vienna. It immediately came into the British orchestral repertory, Manns performing it at the Crystal Palace.

First Movement.

The Movement opens mysteriously with eight bars of unaccompanied melody by 'Cellos and Double-basses in octaves. Though apparently only having here an introductory function, this phrase is really the very soul of the Movement; for it is this phrase that takes us to the emotional heights of the Development Section and Coda (see p. 151).

Immediately the First Subject proper opens as follows:

[1] For details of recordings see p. 153.

And over this as accompaniment there soon creeps in a pathetic and almost despairing melody, which forms the principal feature of the subject. It begins as follows:

Oboe and Clarinet.

The combination of Oboe and Clarinet in unison, in which this melody is given out, is typical of Schubert, who apparently liked the way in which the acid of the first and the sweetness of the second partially neutralized one another.

This melody concluded (the passage closes with 2 bars of Full Orchestra), we come to a lovely link given to 2 Horns and 2 Bassoons (probably simply because Schubert thought he was not very likely to find 4 Horns available anywhere):

Horn and Bassoon.

fp *pp*

which connects it rather naïvely, but effectively, with the **Second Subject.**

This is a cheerful, flowing melody for 'Cellos:

This is simply accompanied by a syncopated chordal accompaniment in Clarinets and Violas, with Double-basses *pizzicato*.

A little later the melody is taken over by First and Second Violins in octaves, and Clarinets, Bassoons, and Horns play the syncopated chords.

Soon there comes an abrupt break (H.M.V. here turns over when repeating the Enunciation), and the mood becomes more strenuous. Note how the Second Subject is discussed, with a touch of passion, which gives way to very tender feeling. The Enunciation closes with a slow descent of Strings *pizzicato* against held Wood-wind octaves. (Parlophone and Polydor end Side One here, Parlophone strangely omitting three bars of link.)

In the Development Section, which follows, a great deal of tragic feeling is expressed by means of an extended treatment of the opening theme (originally taken by bass strings—now given to various instruments, including Trombones). This section is very strenuous. Emotionally it represents the climax of the Movement.

The Recapitulation (Side Three on H.M.V. and Polydor) gives the same material as the Enunciation, with little change that need be mentioned. (Parlophone's Third Side begins with the Horns-Bassoons link to the Second Subject.)

The descending String *pizzicato* passage comes again, and after it a Coda, a final treatment of the gloomy opening theme.

Second Movement.

After the tragic intensity of the First Movement the serenity of the Second is welcome.

It opens very quietly with another chordal phrase for two Horns, two Bassoons (a *pizzicato* Double-bass descending passage under it). Then immediately follows a charming four-bar accompanied melody for Strings alone.

The chordal phrase and the melody are then both repeated.

The whole of the First Subject section grows out of this material. Note a curving *motif* which soon appears and thereafter haunts the Movement. Note also much lovely work by the Wood-wind.

Then, after a new and mysterious four-bar link for First Violin alone, the **Second Subject** enters. It much resembles that of the previous movement, in that a syncopated accompaniment figure is first introduced and a melody then superposed. This melody is long-drawn and lovely:

(Parlophone First Side ends here.)

It is repeated by Oboe, who adds at the end an expressive little phrase, which is softly echoed by Flute, and (fading still further away) again by Oboe.

Suddenly Full Orchestra breaks forth, the sensitive Second Subject hardly recognizable in its declamation by the whole orchestral bass, including the three Trombones.

Then (Polydor and H.M.V. starting their Second Sides) this same melody, turning sensitive again, scales greater heights and sounds greater depths of expression than ever. (Though, to some it may seem, in losing some restraint it has also lost some of its first almost supernatural suggestiveness.)

By and by, the First Subject returns, and we start the Recapitulation. In this there are many significant little changes; the Second Subject, for instance, is given out this time by Oboe, and repeated by Clarinet, and the little phrase at its end is echoed by Oboe, then by Flute. The loud Tutti again follows, now beginning the Coda, which seems loath to bid farewell to the First Subject.

The mysterious Violin introduction to the Second Subject twice appears; but now it has each time to give way to the First Subject in a Wind sextet (first Clarinets, Bassoons and Bass Trombone, then Flutes, Clarinets and Horns).

With the haunting curving *motif* and string *pizzicatos* the piece slowly dies away.

Three Large Parlophone Records. E. 10052–4, 4*s*. 6*d*. each. The Orchestra of the State Opera House, Berlin, conducted by Edward Moerike.

Three Large Polydor Records. 69778–80, 5*s*. 9*d*. each. Orchestra of the State Opera, Berlin, conducted by Otto Klemperer.

Three Large H.M.V. Records. D. 934–6, 6*s*. 6*d*. each. The Royal Albert Hall Orchestra, conducted by Sir Landon Ronald.

Choice between these three recordings must, I think, be decided according to which Movement one values most. (If you wish to get separate recordings of the two Movements you will have to duplicate part of each, getting four records instead of three.)

In incisive playing, telling effect, good Woodwind, fine *Tuttis*, and firm, clear recording, H.M.V. is the best. But they don't get enough dynamic contrast—we never hear a real *pp* until the Second Subject of the Second Movement, which is excellent.

Altogether Parlophone gives the best interpretation, taking the Symphony as a whole. Polydor, on the other hand, gives easily the best interpretation of the Second Movement, very nearly expressing the full beauty of the piece. But in the First Movement Polydor tends to go to sleep, and has some foggy tone, though it has its points (especially dynamic), and satisfies those who like their Second Subject distinctly slow. None of the Records has a perfect surface. Polydor's is the worst.

There is another **Polydor** recording (69597–9, 5*s*. 9*d*. each), but it is inferior all round to the one I have included. On the other hand, on the reverse of the last Record it gives Grieg's Overture, *In Autumn*, very fairly played and recorded.

Those Unheard are Sweeter.

Heard in a London Gramophone Record shop: 'Have you the records of the Unwritten Symphony?'

Printed Music. Miniature Full Score, Goodwin & Tabb, 3*s.* Piano Solo, Augener, No. 8392 a, 2*s.*; Piano Duet, Augener, No. 8217 a, 2*s.* 6*d.*

RECORD No. 56

Two String Quartet Movements { *Andante from String Quartet in D minor* Schubert
Finale from Quartet in G . . . Mozart

THE LÉNER QUARTET.

Schubert. *Andante from Quartet in D minor.*

The Quartet from which this Movement is taken is one of the many posthumous works of Schubert—posthumous as far as publication is concerned, though it was played in public in January 1826, nearly two years before his death. It finely represents his most mature period. It is frequently called the '*Death and the Maiden*' Quartet, from the fact that this Movement is founded upon the elegiac introduction of the composer's song of that name, here, in a slightly extended and developed form, used as the Air for a very expressive set of Variations.

The character of the song will be seen from the following free translation:

The Maiden. Pass by me, Death, thou fearsome shade,
I am but young, a tender maid,
Must I so soon in earth be laid?

Death. Nay, give thine hand, I love thee well,
Take me as friend, Come with me dwell;
And say to every care farewell.

The Air begins:

It is throughout very deep and restrained, lies in a low register, has a compass of but six notes, and takes a good deal of its remarkable beauty from the simple but effective harmony with which Schubert has clothed it. Note the remarkable effect of the change from minor to major in the last two bars—like the letting in of a flood of light as the curtains are drawn after a funeral, or the peace that steals into the mind as, after sadness, a happier thought enters.

Variation I. Air, for the most part in second Violin. Light three-note quaver arpeggio *motif* and two-note descending semiquaver *motif* in First Violin. *Pizzicato* 'Cello. Harmonies as in original Air. (Listen for the Air, as at first the First Violin decorative passage is apt to take the ear.) In the second part of the Variation the First Violin part becomes more florid.

Variation II. A flowing slow tune in the 'Cello, in a high register. This may be looked on as a variant of the original Air, and the harmonies (the real bass now lying in the Viola part, which crosses below the 'Cello) are much as at first:

Thomas Dunhill, in his *Chamber Music: a Treatise for Students*, remarks upon the subtle blending of rhythms supporting a tenor melody sung by the 'Cello, and says :

'The listener is not conscious of any complexity in the accompaniment here. It is more elaborate on paper than in sound. The distinctive characteristics of each part are maintained with unbroken fluency throughout the entire Variation, and there is at no point any sense of effort to maintain the easy flow of the music.'

From here onward there is in the Record a lengthy 'cut', the performance passing to the very touching twenty bars of Coda.

The whole Movement is a piece of very sensitive expression on the part of the composer, sensitively reproduced by the performers.

Mozart. *Finale from Quartet in G* (Köchel, No. 387).

This happy Movement exhibits a curious and successful blend of Sonata Form and Fugue Form.

Enunciation. A mass of interesting matter, mostly contrapuntally treated, may be looked upon as constituting the First Subject.

It begins with a strictly written Fugal Exposition, with Fugal Subject and Countersubject as follows :

Fugue Subject and Countersubject pass through the hands of all the players.

Then follows what is, in effect, a jovial Hornpipe (cf. Haydn's 'Hornpipe' Quartet, page 97 of this book). For six bars this is played by First Violin, then (though the ear hardly recognizes the difference) the Second Violin takes it. The Viola begins, but has it quickly snatched out of its hands and given to the 'Cello.

Other matter follows, and then comes a further Fugal Exposition upon this subject (taken in turn by 'Cello, Violin, Second Violin, and First Violin):

Whilst this still continues, the previous Fugal Subject (the one with which the Movement opened) creeps in, and the two are cleverly treated together. (If you care to study this passage in detail, slow the Gramophone down and listen keenly, over and over again.)

Then enters the Second Subject of the Sonata Form.[1] It begins in this way, in the First Violin, the other instruments supplying the merest accompaniment:

Development. At the outset a six-note rising chromatic scale, given in turn to different instruments, in a very modulatory way. Then the opening Fugal Subject, alternately in First Violin and 'Cello; all for a time very chromatic. Then the Hornpipe tune again; bandied about much as before.

Recapitulation. Then comes the combination of the two Fugal Subjects again, which we may take as opening the Recapitulation.

[1] A piece like this discovers to us the impropriety of the customary use of the word 'Subject' for two very different things, the short melodic theme of a Fugal Exposition and the extended and full harmonized themes of a Sonata Enunciation.

Then the melodious Second Subject (transposed from its former Dominant Key into the Tonic).

Lastly, a Coda made out of the rising six-note chromatic Scale figure and the First Fugal Subject.

All very bright and enjoyable!

Large Columbia Record. L. 1460, 6*s.* 6*d.*

Printed Music. The Mozart Movement is from the Quartet numbered one in Goodwin & Tabb's miniature scores (1*s.* 6*d.*); the Schubert Movement is from the posthumous Quartet in D minor, No. 6, and often called *Death and the Maiden* (same edition, 1*s.* 6*d.*).

The Song *Death and the Maiden* will be found in vol. ii of *Schubert Songs*, published by Novello (2*s.* 6*d.*), and in many similar selections. (A very fine Record of it, made by Elena Gerhardt, has recently been issued by the Vocalion Company.)

Note to Second Edition. The Schubert Air and Variations are now recorded COMPLETE on two sides of a **Large Polydor** Record (66210, 5*s.* 9*d.*) by the Leipzig Gewandhaus String Quartet.

RECORD No. 57

Song . . . . . . *Erlkönig*[1] . . . . . Schubert

Erlkönig.

Wer reitet so spät durch Nacht und Wind?
Es ist der Vater mit seinem Kind;
Er hat den Knaben wohl in dem Arm,
Er fasst ihn sicher, er hält ihn warm.

'Mein Sohn, was birgst du so bang dein Gesicht?'—
'Siehst, Vater, du den Erlkönig nicht?
Den Erlenkönig mit Kron' und Schweif?'—
'Mein Sohn, es ist ein Nebelstreif.'—

'Du liebes Kind, komm, geh mit mir!
Gar schöne Spiele spiel' ich mit dir,
Manch bunte Blumen sind an dem Strand,
Meine Mutter hat manch gülden Gewand.'

'Mein Vater, mein Vater, und hörest du nicht,
Was Erlenkönig mir leise verspricht?'—
'Sei ruhig, bleibe ruhig, mein Kind:
In dürren Blättern säuselt der Wind.'—

'Willst, feiner Knabe, du mit mir gehn?
Meine Töchter sollen dich warten schön;
Meine Töchter führen den nächtlichen Reihn
Und wiegen und tanzen und singen dich ein.'

'Mein Vater, mein Vater, und siehst du nicht dort
Erlkönigs Töchter am düstern Ort?'—
'Mein Sohn, mein Sohn, ich seh' es genau:
Es scheinen die alten Weiden so grau.'—

'Ich liebe dich, mich reizt deine schöne Gestalt;
Und bist du nicht willig, so brauch' ich Gewalt.'—
'Mein Vater, mein Vater, jetzt fasst er mich an!
Erlkönig hat mir ein Leids getan.'

[1] For singers see p. 164.

Dem Vater grauset's, er reitet geschwind,
Er hält in den Armen das ächzende Kind,
Erreicht den Hof mit Müh und Not;
In seinen Armen das Kind war tot.

THE ERL-KING.

Sir Walter Scott's translation.

O, who rides by night thro' the woodland so wild?
It is the fond father, embracing his child;
And close the boy nestles within his loved arm,
To hold himself fast, and to keep himself warm.

'O father, see yonder! see yonder!' he says;
'My boy, upon what dost thou fearfully gaze?'—
'O, 'tis the Erl-King with his crown and his shroud.'
'No, my son, it is but a dark wreath of the cloud.'

Erl-King.

*'O come and go with me, thou loveliest child;
By many a gay sport shall thy time be beguiled;
My mother keeps for thee full many a fair toy,
And many a fine flower shall she pluck for my boy.'*

'O father, my father, and did you not hear
The Erl-King whisper so low in my ear?'—
'Be still, my heart's darling—my child, be at ease;
It was but the wild blast as it sung thro' the trees.'

Erl-King.

*'O wilt thou go with me, thou loveliest boy?
My daughter shall tend thee with care and with joy;
She shall bear thee so lightly thro' wet and thro' wild,
And press thee, and kiss thee, and sing to my child.'*

'O father, my father, and saw you not plain
The Erl-King's pale daughter glide by thro' the rain?'—
'O yes, my loved treasure, I know it full soon;
It was the grey willow that danced to the moon.'

Erl-King.

*'O come and go with me, no longer delay,
Or else, silly child, I will drag thee away.'*
'O father! O father! now, now, keep your hold,
The Erl-King has seized me—his grasp is so cold!'—

Sore trembled the father; he spurr'd thro' the wild,
Clasping close to his bosom his shuddering child;
He reaches his dwelling in doubt and in dread,
But, clasp'd to his bosom, the infant was *dead*!

The following description of the circumstances of the composition of this song are taken from A. D. Coleridge's translation of von Hellborn's *Life of Schubert:*

'According to Josef v. Spaun, it was in the last days of 1815, or at the latest in the beginning of the year 1816, that the "Erl-King" was written, second only in point of popularity to the 'Wanderer' in the solid foundation of Schubert's popularity six years later, and which, within a short time, became the property of the whole musical world. Schubert wrote this song one afternoon in his room in his father's house in Himmelpfortgrund. Spaun came to see him whilst he was hard at work. He had read the poem twice in a state of intense mental excitement, and as, whilst thus employed, the musical significance of the poem had dawned upon him, he had dashed down on a paper a sketch which only needed some mechanical finish to bring to perfection. On the evening of the same day his composition was brought finished to the Konvikt, where Schubert sang it over first, and then Holzapfel to his friends. The audience made wry faces, and smiled incredulously at the passage, "Mein Vater, jetzt fasst er mich an," whereupon Ruczizka undertook to clear up the mystery and explain the discords, which nowadays are reckoned so harmless an incident to music. As Vogl was intimate with Schubert, he immediately monopolized this song, which seemed created on purpose for his particular powers, and sang it on frequent occasions in private society, until at last, in the year 1821, on the occasion of an academy being opened at the Royal Opera, the "Erl-King" was introduced to the general public.'

There is on record a private performance of this song in which the parts of Father, Erl-King, and Boy were taken by three singers, Schubert himself taking that of the Erl-King.

The success of 'Erlkönig' did much to establish Schubert's reputation. Yet it had to be published by a subscription amongst the composer's friends, as the publishers would not touch it. Quite possibly the difficulty of the accompaniment had something to do with the hesitation of these business men; it is a factor they still take into account, as composers to-day are well aware.

Large Polydor Record. Hermann Jadlowker. 72678, 6*s.* 9*d.* On the reverse, Liszt's *Der Fischerknabe* (*The Fisher-boy*) with orchestra.

Large Vocalion Record. Roy Henderson (in English), accompanied by Stanley Chapple. K. 05167, 4*s.* 6*d.* On the reverse, Schubert's *Serenade.*

Large Polydor Record. Heinrich Rehkemper. 66006, 5*s.* 9*d.* On the reverse, Schubert's *Orpheus.*

Large Vocalion Record. Elena Gerhardt, accompanied by Ivor Newton. A. 0215, 5*s.* 6*d.* On the reverse, Schumann's *Der Nussbaum* (*The Walnut-tree* or *The Hazel-tree*).

Jadlowker, in German, is very fine indeed, and Henderson, in English, almost as good. But the other two Records (both in German) are also extremely good (excepting that Gerhardt has here rather a bad *tremolo*, and that *The Erl-King* seems preferably a man's song); and if one wishes the song in German and has special preference for any one of the songs on the reverse, that preference may be allowed to decide one's choice.

On the reverse sides Jadlowker gives us a fairly interesting Liszt song, Henderson Schubert's popular Serenade, Rehkemper another Schubert of no really outstanding worth, and Gerhardt a fairly popular Schumann song which represents its composer in very charming, if rather sentimental mood.

Printed Music. The song will be found in almost any volume of Schubert's songs, e.g. (in German) in the Peters Edition, 'Schubert-Album', Vol. 1 (No. 8846, 7*s.* 6*d.*), or (in English) in Novello's 'Schubert Songs', Vol. 3 (3*s.*). See 'Printed Music', p. 148.

GLOSSARY AND LIST OF COMPOSERS

WITH an Explanation of all Technical Terms used in this Book or on the labels of the Records mentioned, Pronunciation of Foreign or Obsolete Words, Dates of Composers, &c.

Acciaccatura (atch-i-ak-a-*too*-ra). A very short 'grace' note, usually immediately above or below the one it ornaments.

Adagio Sostenuto (ad-*ahj*-ee-oh sos-ten-*oo*-toh). Slow and sustained (i.e. slow and smooth).

Adagio Cantabile (ad-*ahj*-ee-oh can-*tah*-bee-lay). Slow and in a singing style.

Allegretto (al-ay-*gret*-to). Rather lively (diminutive of 'Allegro').

Allegro (al-*ay*-gro). Lively.

Allegro con brio (al-*ay*-gro con *bree*-o). Lively, with spirit.

Allemande (al-e[*r*]-mande). See p. 21 for a description.

Alto = 'high'. The highest (generally 'falsetto') man's voice. Used to denote instruments and music of that pitch, also loosely used as = *Contr*-alto (q.v.). Cf. S.A.T.B.

Andante (an-*dan*-ty). Literally 'going', with the implication of moving along steadily; neither fast nor slow, but rather slow than fast.

Andante con Moto (an-*dan*-ty con *moh*-toh). Literally 'going, with movement', rather faster than 'Andante'.

Andante con Variazioni (an-*dan*-ty con vah-ree-atz-ee-*ohn*-ee). For 'Andante' see above. 'Con variazioni' indicates that the (Andante) 'Air' is followed by a series of variations.

Andante Sostenuto (an-*dan*-ty sos-ten-*oo*-toh). Andante (q.v.) and in a *sustained* style, i.e. smoothly.

Answer. In a Fugue (q.v.), = the form in which the Subject is presented by the second Voice to enter, which Voice has the effect of *answering* the Voice which led off.

Arabesque. An ornamental figure in melody, much the equivalent in tone of the arabesque in linear design.

Arpeggio (ar-*pedge*-ee-oh). Chord of which the notes are played not simultaneously, but successively, *harp*-fashion (Arpa = Harp).

Bach (Bahk—approximately), **John Sebastian** (1685–1750). For an account of his life, work, and influence, with bibliography and particulars of further Gramophone Records of his music, see *The Listener's History of Music*, i, pp. 96–102.

Ballett. See pp. 7–8. A Madrigal in dance rhythm and style.

Bar (or, perhaps better, **Measure**). In the more rigidly metrical music since the later seventeenth century, is, broadly speaking, the time unit into which strong and weak accents are grouped.

Bass. The lowest in pitch of all the varieties of the human voice, or the lowest instrument engaged in a piece, or the 'part' sung or played by that voice or instrument.

Bassoon. The bass Oboe (q. v.). For a picture of it see *The Listener's Guide*, frontispiece, or *The First Book of the Great Musicians*, p. 78.

Bateson, Thomas (*c*. 1570–1630).

Beethoven (*Bayt*-hoh-ven), **Ludwig van** (1770–1827). For an account of his life, works and influence, a bibliography and particulars of further Gramophone Records, see *The Listener's History of Music*, i, pp. 159–63, and elsewhere in the same volume.

Bennet (or **Bennett**), **John.** Sixteenth and early seventeenth century, precise dates unknown. For a short note on him see *The Listener's History of Music*, i, p. 48.

Binary. In two parts. For an example of a piece in *Simple Binary* form see the description of a Bach Allemande on p. 21, that of a Purcell

Sarabande, on pp. 27–8, and other examples in the earlier part of this book. *Compound Binary Form* (so called for historical reasons since it is an outgrowth from Simple Binary, but really a Ternary form) is the same as 'Sonata Form' (q.v.).

Bourrée (boo-ray). See p. 34.

Bridge. A connecting passage, generally applied to that between the First and Second Subjects in a Movement in 'Sonata Form'. See p. 80, &c.

Broken Chord, much the same as Arpeggio (q.v.).

Bull, John (*c.* 1562–1628). For an account of his life and work see *The Listener's History of Music*, i, p. 46.

Byrd, William (1543–1623). For a short account of his life and works see *The Listener's History of Music*, i, p. 45.

Cadence (or Close). A point of rest in a piece, such as the two chords which bring it to an end, or those which, occurring at the end of some Phrase, provide a momentary sensasation of rest. Thus Cadences are the punctuation of music, corresponding nearly to commas and full stops.

Cadenza. See an example of a very short one on p. 135. In a Concerto the Cadenza is a display passage left to the solo player, and often of considerable length.

Capriccio (cap-*reach*-ee-o). Caprice, a short piece of instrumental music of the character suggested by the word.

'Cello (*tchel*-lo) = Violoncello (q.v.).

Chamber Music. Properly any music suitable for performance in a domestic room, as distinct from Orchestral Music, Opera, and Oratorio. Actually applied to Sonatas for two instruments (*not* usually to those for one), instrumental Trios, Quartets, &c.

Choral. For a Choir.

Chord. A combination of notes sounded together.

Chordal = Constructed in Chords.

Chromatic. Proceeding by Semitones, as, for instance, the Chromatic Scale, which, on the Pianoforte, takes in all the notes, white and black, in succession.

Clarinet. A Wood-wind instrument, at first sight somewhat like the Oboe, but of smoother tone. For a picture of it see *The Listener's Guide*, frontispiece, or *The First Book of the Great Musicians*, p. 78.

Clavier (clav-*eer*). Properly any keyed instrument, but usually (as on p. 49) used for Harpsichord or Clavichord, i.e. excluding Organ and Piano. In German 'Klavier' is now used for 'Pianoforte'.

Coda (*coh*-da). Literally a 'tail', i.e. an additional portion at the end of a Movement or piece, serving to give it satisfactory and final-sounding conclusion.

Concerto (con-*chair*-toh). See p. 44.

Continuo (con-*teen*-oo-oh). Figured Bass (q.v.).

Contralto. The deeper type of woman's voice, or, alternatively, the woman herself. (Schoolboy definition: 'Contralto—a woman who sings low songs.')

Contrapuntal. In the manner of Counterpoint (q.v.).

Corant, Courante (cor-*ant*, coo-*rant*). A dance piece in three-beat time, found as a constituent member of the eighteenth-century Suite. See pp. 21 and 28.

Counterpoint (cf. 'Melody' and 'Harmony'). A combination of melodies performed simultaneously.

Countersubject. See under 'Fugue', and for an example see p. 63.

Couperin (Coop-er-an, approximately), **François** (1668–1737). For a short account of his life and work see *The Listener's History of Music*, i, pp. 102–3.

Cres., Crescendo (cres-*shen*-doh). Increasing gradually in volume of tone.

Decrescendo (day-cres-*shen*-doh). Decreasing gradually in volume of tone.

Development. See p. 133.

Dim., Diminuendo (dee-meen-oo-*en*-doh) = decrescendo (q.v.).

Division. See p. 12.
Dolce (*dol*-chay). Sweetly (with the implication, softly).
Dominant. The fifth degree of a major or minor key. Thus, in the key of C the Dominant is G.
Double-bass. The largest instrument of the bowed-string class.
Double-bassoon. (See p. 141.) A Bassoon (q.v.) with a range an octave below that of the normal instrument, and so standing in relation to that much as a Double-bass to a 'Cello.
Doubles. Variations.

Edwards, Richard (*c.* 1523-66). For a short note on his life and works see *The Listener's History of Music*, i, p. 50.
Ensemble. (French = 'together'.) The blending into artistic unity of the performance of two or more performers. The body of performers itself.
Entry. See under 'Fugue'.
Enunciation. See p. 133.
Exposition. See under 'Fugue'. Also = Enunciation.

Fantasia or **Fantazia** (fan-taz-*ee*-a). Properly any composition in a free, fanciful form. As the term was used in the sixteenth and seventeenth centuries (see reference on p. 18) it meant a contrapuntal composition with a good deal of imitation—practically a rudimentary form of Fugue.
Farmer, John (*c.* 1565–1605). For a short note upon him see *The Listener's History of Music*, i, p. 50.
Figured Bass. See pp. 32 and 51.
First-Movement Form. See p. 133.
Flute. The Wood-wind instrument familiar to all, held horizontally to the player's right—the glorified whistle.
f. or **forte** (*for*-ty) = loudly.
fortissimo (for-*tees*-eem-oh) = very loudly.
Forty-eight, The. A collection of forty-eight Preludes and Fugues by Bach, in two books, each containing a Prelude and Fugue in each of the twelve Major and twelve Minor Keys.
Fugal. In the fugue style.
Fugue. A contrapuntal composition in some fixed number of parts, or Voices, as they are called (even in an instrumental Fugue), of which now one, now another introduces the SUBJECT, a short snatch of melody devised for the purpose.

At the outset the voices enter separately with the Subject, so that at first one Voice alone is heard, then two, and so forth. As this goes on, in many Fugues, the Voice which has just relinquished the Subject continues by taking up a contrasting snatch of melody called the COUNTERSUBJECT.

When all the Voices have made their first ENTRY, the EXPOSITION of the Fugue is complete. Then usually follows an EPISODE, a short passage (usually constructed from some *motif* or *motifs* taken from the material just heard) which leads to further appearances, or Entries of the Subject. Other Episodes and Entries succeed, and so, at last, bring the Fugue to an end.

As just set forth, the Fugue appears as an ingenious manner of effectively developing a more or less lengthy piece of music from a small amount of original material. It should be added that from another point of view it may be looked upon as an ingenious use of the principle of Contrast of Key. In the Exposition, the first appearance of the Subject is, naturally, in the main (or 'Tonic') Key of the piece, but the next appearance is in the Key of five notes higher (or the Dominant Key, as it is termed), and subsequent appearances during the Exposition alternate between these two keys.

The Exposition ended, the first Episode usually leads into some related Key, in which the next Entry takes place, and further Episodes and Entries similarly introduce further related Keys.

A device sometimes employed is that of PEDAL (q.v.), and another, that of STRETTO (q.v.).

Galliard (*gal*-ee-ard). See p. 18. An old dance, for two dancers, in triple time—practically an early Minuet.

Gavotte. See p. 34.

Gibbons, Orlando (1583-1625). For a short account of him see *The Listener's History of Music*, i, p. 52.

Gigue (something between 'jeeg' and 'sheeg') = Jig. A lively dance form in three, six, nine, or twelve-beat time, which formed one of the movements of the old Suites. See p. 21.

G String. The fourth, or lowest, string of the Violin. See p 49.

Half-close. A Cadence (q.v.) formed of two chords, of which the latter is the Dominant Chord, giving an inconclusive effect, and hence often used in the middle of a composition.

Handel, George Frederick (1685-1759). For an account of his life and work, a bibliography and list of further Gramophone Records, &c., see *The Listener's History of Music*, i, pp. 94-6 and 100-2.

Harmony (cf. 'Melody' and 'Counterpoint'). A combination of notes performed simultaneously.

Harpsichord. The precursor of the Pianoforte. As the keys were depressed the strings were plucked (not hammered, as in the Pianoforte). A full description of the Harpsichord (with pictures and diagrams) will be found in *The Third Book of the Great Musicians*, Chapter V, and a briefer one in *The Listener's History of Music*, i, Appendix V.

Haydn, Franz Joseph (1732-1809). For an account of life and works, bibliography and list of further Gramophone Records, &c., see *The Listener's History of Music*, i, pp. 153-5.

Horn. A brass instrument, capable either of very gentle, smooth tone, when played softly, or of almost blatant tone when played loudly. For a picture see *The Listener's Guide*, p. 64, or *The First Book of the Great Musicians*, p. 78.

Imitation. In contrapuntal music, the taking up by one 'voice' of some snatch of tune that has just been performed by another.

In Nomine (In *nom*-in-ey). Literally 'In the Name', a sort of Motet, or Anthem, or free Choral Fugue, to Latin words. This rather curious term was used in the sixteenth and seventeenth centuries — probably originally for settings of words which began 'In nomine Jesu', and the like. Also used for instrumental pieces.

Inversion. See p. 56. Also p. 47—another use.

Kettledrum = Timpani. The only drums tuned to definite pitch. There are at least two in every Full Orchestra.

Key. The principle of selection, by which seven notes are chosen (out of the twelve available) as the material out of which a passage is to be constructed or mainly constructed. The notes of a Key, arranged in consecutive order, constitute the scale of that Key. See explanation, with diagrams, of the Key systems, in *The Listener's Guide to Music.*

Larghetto (larg-*et*-toh). Not quite so slow as 'Largo' (q.v.).

Largo. Literally 'wide, broad'. Slow and stately.

Largo, ma non tanto. Slow and dignified, but not too much so.

Madrigal (*mad*-ri-gal). The secular choral form of the late sixteenth and early seventeenth centuries—usually very contrapuntal in character.

Major, minor. Keys are 'major' or 'minor' according to the order of tones and semitones. The major is generally supposed to be the brighter, but see Records 15-17.

Measure = Bar, q.v.

Melody (cf. 'Harmony' and 'Counterpoint'). A series of notes performed in succession, in such a way as to make a 'tune'.

Minuet. A dance form, with three beats in each bar, common in the seventeenth and eighteenth centuries. See pp. 29, 79–80, 89–90, and 96. The Minuet was a frequent member of the Suite and the eighteenth-century Sonata, String Quartet, Symphony, &c. With Beethoven and later writers, it was frequently replaced by a more lively Movement, the Scherzo (q.v.).

Modes. The old key system, gradually superseded in the seventeenth century. For a simple explanation see the special chapter in *The Listener's History of Music*, vol. i.

Modulation. Change of key during the course of a piece. See p. 73.

Molto. Much (e.g. molto allegro, &c.).

Motif (moh-*teef*), also spelt Motive. A short theme, or portion of a theme. Roughly speaking, when a 'Subject', or musical theme, has been divided into its smallest intelligible portions, these are the *Motifs* of that Subject or Theme.

Movement. Any one of the several separate pieces which collectively make up such a piece as a Sonata, a String Quartet, a Symphony, &c.

Mozart (*Mote*-sart), **Wolfgang Amadeus** (1756–91). For an account of his life and work, bibliography, list of further Gramophone Records, &c., see *The Listener's History of Music*, i, pp. 156–9.

Obbligato (ob-lee-*gah*-toh). An instrumental part of essential importance to the effect of the composition. (The composers of 'cheap' songs and the like nowadays use it in the contrary sense, applying it to an optional part.)

Oboe (*oh*-boh). A Wood-wind instrument, of pleasant acid tone, not so smooth as that of the Clarinet. For a picture see *The Listener's Guide*, frontispiece, or *The First Book of the Great Musicians*, p. 78.

Octave (8ve). Distance or span of 8 notes. It is universally recognized (and supported by physical law) that in a scale the notes begin, at the eighth note, to reproduce themselves at a higher or lower pitch.

Octuplet. A group of eight notes played within one beat.

Oratorio. A large-scale work for Solo Voice, Chorus and Orchestra; properly a sacred work, but the word was loosely used in the eighteenth century. For the history of the Oratorio see *The Listener's History of Music*, vol. i.

Orchestration. That portion of the process of composition which consists in the allotting of the functions of the various instruments of the Orchestra—akin to the colouring of a picture, already (actually or mentally) drawn.

Ornament. See p. 29.

Overture. Properly, the introductory music to an Oratorio, Opera or other large musical work, or to a Play. Sometimes simply indicates an independent opening piece.

p. = piano, softly.

Partita (par-*tee*-ta). A Suite (q.v.). See pp. 20–1.

Pastorale (pas-tor-*ahl*-ay). In the pastoral style—which generally implies rather slow music with six or twelve beats in a bar, in the manner of certain shepherd melodies of Italy (cf. Handel's 'Pastoral Symphony' in the *Messiah*).

Pavan or Pavane (Pa-*van*). A stately dance of the sixteenth and seventeenth centuries, which suggested the style of a good deal of keyboard music of the period (in this connexion often linked to the Galliard, q.v.).

Pedal (as a term in Harmony). See pp. 37 and 54.

Phrase. A small section of music, corresponding very much to a line in a verse of poetry. All music will be found, on close listening, to consist of a succession of short phrases.

Piano, or p. (pee-*ahn*-oh). Softly.

Pianissimo (pee-ahn-*eess*-ee-moh). Very softly.

Piccolo (*pick*-oh-loh). A small Flute (the word *piccolo* is Italian for 'small'). For a picture of it see *The Listener's Guide*, frontispiece, and *The First Book of the Great Musicians*, p. 78.

Pizzicato (pits-ee-*cah*-toh) (of Stringed Instruments), 'plucked' instead of bowed.
pp. Pianissimo (q.v.).
Prelude. Properly, a piece intended as an introduction to some other piece or pieces, as for instance 'Prelude and Fugue' (see p. 53). Sometimes, however, independent Preludes are now composed.
Presto (*press*-toh). Quick.
Purcell, Henry (1658 or 1659–95). For an account of his life and work see *The Listener's History of Music*, i, pp. 91–3.

Quartet. A piece for four (single) Voices, or for four Instruments, or those combinations themselves. A String Quartet consists of two Violins, Viola and Violoncello, and a Piano Quartet of Violin, Viola, Violoncello, and Piano.
Quasi (*quah*-zee). Almost; as if.

Rameau, Jean-Philippe (1683–1764). For a short account of his life and work see *The Listener's History of Music*, i, pp. 103–4.
Recapitulation. See p. 134.
Recitative (res-ee-tat-*eev*). In the speaking style. See p. 73.
Relative Major / **" Minor** } The Major and Minor Keys which possess the same Key-signature, e.g. C Major and A Minor, G Major and E Minor. That they are actually 'relatives' is shown by the fact that modulation from one to the other is very easily accomplished and sounds very natural.
Rhythm. The element in music of stresses, and of varying lengths of note, from which element much of the vitality of a piece depends.
Rondo or **Rondeau.** See p. 34.

Sarabande (sa-ra-band). See p. 27.
S.A.T.B. A choral combination consisting of Soprano, Alto, Tenor, and Bass, i.e. the normal constitution of mixed-voice Choirs.
Scale. See 'Key'.
Scarlatti, Domenico (1685–1757). For an account of his life and works, and lists of further Gramophone Records, see *The Listener's History of Music*, i, pp. 105–6.
Scherzo (*skair*-tso). Literally, a joke. A lively piece, which, as one of the middle movements of a Sonata, Symphony, or piece of Chamber Music, was originally developed (by Beethoven) out of the Minuet.
Schubert, Franz (1797–1828). For an account of his life and works see *The Listener's History of Music*, i, pp. 163–6.
Score (Full). A setting forth of the music which shows the 'parts' for all the instruments, voices, &c., simultaneously. A 'Piano Score' is a reduction of all this to a Piano 'arrangement'.
Semitone. The smallest difference of pitch recognized in normal music, e.g. that between any two contiguous notes (without distinction of black or white) on the piano.
Sequence, Sequential. See p. 70.
Sextolet. A group of six notes performed within one beat.
Sf. or **Sforzando** (sforts-*an*-doh), forced, i.e. strongly accented (applied to the performance of particular single notes or chords).
Sonata. See pp. 31, 67, and 117. Also study the description of any of the (complete) String Quartets mentioned in this book, or of the Beethoven Fifth Symphony, which are all Sonatas, though not so called (the name being subsequently restricted to a piece of this style for one instrument or two instruments).
Sonata Form. First Movement Form. See p. 133.
Song cycle. (p. 146.) A series of songs intended to be sung consecutively.
Soprano (sop-*rah*-noh). The highest in pitch of all human voices.
Sostenuto (sos-ten-*oo*-toh). Sustained = smoothly.
S.S.A.T.B. A choral combination consisting of two Sopranos, Alto, Tenor, and Bass.
Staccato (stac-*cah*-toh). Detached. Applied to notes that are not to be sustained for their full value. Often

indicated by the placing of dots or dashes over notes.

Stretto. See p. 53.

Subject. In the case of *Fugue*, a mere snatch of melody which serves as the material out of which the composition is largely constructed (see under 'Fugue'). In the case of a *Sonata Movement*, one of the more or less extended passages, fully harmonized, which are in themselves, at the opening and closing section of the movement, an important part of the material of this, and which, disintegrated, supply the material from which the middle section is 'developed' (see under 'Sonata').

Suite. A string of short pieces (originally mostly in dance rhythms), so arranged as to form one long and well-varied piece. See pp. 20-21 and 28 and 29.

Symphony. A Sonata for full Orchestra.

Syncopation. Displacement of the accent, as, for instance, is done in rag-time (an extreme case).

Tabor. A small drum used rurally (in conjunction with the Pipe) in the sixteenth and seventeenth centuries. See p. 36.

Tambourin (tam-boo-ran, approximately). See p. 36.

Tenor. The highest in pitch of natural male voices (this excludes the Alto, which is rarely a natural voice). Also instruments of that pitch, and that pitch itself.

Tenth (see p. 77). The interval between two notes with eight others between them, i.e. a third enlarged by the addition of an octave.

Ternary. See p. 71.

Theme = 'Subject' (q.v.).

Timpani. The Kettledrums (q.v.).

Tomkins, Thos. (*c.* 1573–1656).

Tonality. The sense of Key (q.v.).

Tone. The difference in pitch amounting to two semitones. Also the quality of a musical sound.

Tonic. The principal note of a Key (q.v.). The first note of the scale of that Key (cf. 'Dominant').

Transposition. The alteration of pitch of a passage, without changing it in any other way, in other words, the lifting it bodily out of its original Key (q.v.) into some other.

Trio. Properly, any composition for three voices or instruments; a special meaning, however, is that of the second Minuet, which alternates with the first one in a Suite or work of Sonata class (see p. 80).

Triplet. A group of three notes, played within one beat, or within the usual time of two.

Trombone. A Brass Instrument of lower pitch—the push-out-and-pull-in one. For a picture see *The Listener's Guide to Music*, p. 64, or *The First Book of the Great Musicians*, p. 78.

Trumpet. The familiar treble brass instrument, not to be confused with the shorter, smoother-toned Cornet, often used as a substitute in small bands.

Tutti (*Toot*-ee). See p. 55.

Unison. The playing or singing, by two or more performers, of the same notes as one another, i.e. the mere duplication or multiplication at the same pitch of a note or line of notes. Sometimes = duplication at different pitch.

Variations. See pp. 43, 77–8, 88–9, and 135–8, from which a clear idea of the form will be gathered.

Viola (vee-*oh*-la). A Stringed Instrument a size larger than the Violin and a size smaller than the Violoncello.

Violin. The smallest in size and highest in pitch of the bowed Stringed Instruments. First and Second Violin are identical as instruments, but play different 'parts'.

Violoncello (vee-oh-lon-*chel*-loh). A Stringed Instrument too big to hold to the chin (like the Violin and Viola), and not big enough to require the player to stand behind it (like the Double-bass)—the one, then, which is held between the knees by a sitting performer.

Viols (*vy*-ols). The precursors of the Violin family. They looked very like the members of that family, but had flat backs, 'frets' on the finger-board, to mark the notes, and (usually) six strings, instead of the present four.

Virginals. An early form of the Harpsichord (q.v.).

Vivace (vee-*vah*-chay). Lively.

Voyals. See 'Viols'.

Weelkes, Thomas (1575–1623). For a short note of him see *The Listener's History of Music*, i, p. 55.

Wilbye, John (1574–1638). For a short account of his life see *The Listener's History of Music*, i, p. 56.

Wood-wind. Wind Instruments made of wood, e.g. the Piccolo, Flute, Oboe, Clarinet, Bassoon.

THE READER'S NOTES

(INCLUDING any suggestions he intends to make to the Author for the improvement of this book and others to follow in the same series.)